A Life Inspired

TALES OF PEACE CORPS SERVICE

PEACE CORPS

Paul D. Coverdell Peace Corps Headquarters
1111 20th Street, NW | Washington, DC 20526
www.peacecorps.gov   *800.424.8580*

A Life Inspired: Tales of Peace Corps Service

The opinions expressed in *A Life Inspired: Tales of Peace Corps Service* are those of the authors and do not necessarily reflect the views of the Peace Corps or the government of the United States.

The Peace Corps expresses its appreciation to the current and returned Volunteers for their service and for sharing their experiences in the following stories.

January 2006 · Library of Congress Catalog No. 2005910173

FOR SALE BY THE SUPERINTENDENT OF DOCUMENTS, U.S. GOVERNMENT PRINTING OFFICE
Internet: bookstore.gpo.gov | **Phone:** *Toll-free* (866) 512-1800; *D.C. Area:* (202) 512-1800
Fax: (202) 512-2250   **Mail:** Stop SSOP, Washington, DC 20402-0001

ISBN 0-9644472-6-6
ISBN 978-0-96-444726-7

CONTENTS

Foreword

Making a Difference

Life is Calling

Window to the World

Becoming a Peace Corps Volunteer

LIVING A LIFE INSPIRED
Gaddi Vasquez

As director of the Peace Corps, it has been my honor to visit with thousands of Peace Corps Volunteers all over the world and to see firsthand the remarkable dedication, passion, and skill they bring to serving others. As a member of the community working in an environment of mutual trust and respect, Peace Corps Volunteers strengthen friendships and foster understanding between Americans and people of other countries.

Peace Corps Volunteers are visionaries. They come from all walks of life, range in age from college students to retirees, and reflect the rich diversity of America. They leave the comforts of home and travel thousands of miles to help others in villages, towns, and cities around the globe. The work of Peace Corps Volunteers builds on a legacy that has become a significant part of America's history. Their desire to make a difference has improved the lives of millions of people around the world and at home. The journey takes perseverance, a lot of courage, a capacity for patience, a dose of humor, and an appreciation for living and learning within a different culture. It is a unique person who answers this call.

A Volunteer's work varies according to the needs of each country, but all Volunteers learn to speak the local language and appreciate the culture and values of the people they serve while sharing their unique perspectives on America. When they return home, Volunteers bring not only valuable real-world skills for future endeavors, but also an expanded worldview to share.

The significance of the Peace Corps experience does not diminish over time for Volunteers. Returned Volunteers consistently refer to their time in the Peace Corps as one of the most important influences in the course of their lives' direction—even decades later. This is understandable when considering that the commitment Volunteers make to train and serve in a foreign land for over two years is no small thing. The personal challenges Volunteers face to honor that commitment enriches their lives deeply. The difference they make to the lives of the people they live and work with reverberates for years to come. The rewards of a life enriched through new friends in a culture and country far from home provide life-long bonds and memories.

Each Peace Corps Volunteer's journey holds hundreds of stories. The collection in this book is a brief sampling of living a life inspired.

"*Life in the Peace Corps will not be easy. There will be no salary and allowances will be at a level sufficient only to maintain health and meet basic needs. Men and women will be expected to work and live alongside the nationals of the country in which they are stationed—doing the same work, eating the same food, talking the same language.*

But if the life will not be easy, it will be rich and satisfying. For every young American who participates in the Peace Corps—who works in a foreign land—will know that he or she is sharing in the great common task of bringing to man that decent way of life which is the foundation of freedom and a condition of peace."

JOHN F. KENNEDY
35TH PRESIDENT OF THE UNITED STATES
AND FOUNDER OF THE PEACE CORPS

~~~

WHERE CREDIT IS DUE

Karen Schaefer · Tanzania

"Will you join our club, Mama Karen?"

My friend, Mama Komunte, approached me with this offer shortly after I'd set up house in the village of Mzumbe
in Tanzania. Quite the entrepreneur, she had introduced
herself to me even before I'd officially moved in. During a
brief site visit taken halfway through Peace Corps' in-country training, she had offered me twice-weekly Kiswahili lessons at her home after school, for a small fee. She was in
her 40s, about 10 years younger than me, a mother of four,
friendly, ambitious—and nobody's patsy.

"What club is that?" I said.

"It's the Mzumbe Women Workers' Club."

"And what do you do in your club?" I asked, assuming it
was a social club, something like the "Women Who Read
Too Much Book Club" that I had abandoned when I departed for Tanzania.

"We take dues," Mama Komunte replied.

Several seconds beat by as I waited for her to elaborate. And? I thought. Surely the purpose of the club was not simply to take dues. But nothing followed. When it became clear Mama Komunte had no further explanation, I asked, "So what will you do with the dues?"

"We will give them to one of the club members," Mama Komunte said, as if this should be obvious.

"You will give them to a club member," I repeated. Clearly, I didn't get it.

Mama Komunte looked at me as she might a not-too-swift child. The newly formed Mzumbe Women Workers' Club, she explained, had 13 members, 14 now—she indicated me—all of them teachers or staff at Mzumbe Secondary School. Dues were 2,000 shillings a month. Each month a different club member would receive the lump sum of the one month's entire club dues.

This baffled me. "But you will only be getting your money back," I said. "You could simply save your 2,000 shillings for 14 months and pay yourself the same amount." Was I missing something? Though I had been a high school teacher most of my adult life and knew virtually nothing about business or investing, like most Americans, I had the innate belief that the whole idea behind money was to make it grow.

"Yes, but you don't understand," Mama Komunte continued. "It's not possible for us to save money. If it's in the house, someone will spend it. Our husbands will find it and use it to buy beer or we will need it for school fees or medicine for one of the children. This way, once in a while, we will have some money to buy something nice. Maybe a pretty tablecloth or a new set of dishes."

Still, I couldn't leave it alone. "But you will make no progress," I protested. "You should use the dues money to make more money." True, I hadn't a clue how this could be done, but, even though I was now apparently a member of the club, the whole thing struck me as pointless.

"Come to the meeting tomorrow afternoon," Mama Komunte replied. "Tell us how. You are American. Americans know how to make money. We Tanzanians don't know that. Mama Karen, you must teach us how to be businesswomen."

The next afternoon, after the last class of the day, all 14 members of the Mzumbe Women Workers' Club gathered in the staff room. The first order of business was to appoint officers. Mama Komunte, who had taken it upon herself to run the meeting anyway, was named president. Mama Kihombo, the chemistry teacher, became the club secretary. The school's bookkeeper was appointed treasurer. Dutifully, we all handed her our 2,000 shillings. She recounted it just to be sure. There, in a pile on a scuffed wooden desk, lay 28,000 shillings—close to $50 and nearly a month's salary for an Mzumbe teacher. Now it was time to determine who would be the lucky first recipient. Mama Kihombo, as secretary, wrote the numbers 1 through 14 on slips of paper, carefully folding each one before dropping it into a small basket. One by one, each woman withdrew a folded slip from the basket. Mama Macha, the school librarian, the first to draw, squealed with delight and held high the number two—next month, the pile would be hers.

The high spirits spread as women who drew low numbers beamed at their good fortune and those who drew high numbers laughed at their ill luck.

When the basket reached me, I shook my head. It just didn't seem right to take their money. Logically, of course, I understood it was my money, too, but I had seen how hard these women worked for so little reward. Comparatively, even on my Peace Corps stipend, I possessed a small fortune.

"No, no, Mama Karen," everyone insisted. "You have to take a number. You are a member of the club. Everyone must take a number."

I knew I had no good argument, and reluctantly, I complied. A roomful of eyes fastened on me as I unfolded my slip of paper and held up what I'd drawn—14, the highest possible number. The room pealed with laughter, mine mingling with the rest; I'd be the very last to receive the cash.

Fourteen months passed quickly. What with preparing lessons and teaching classes, studying Kiswahili, winnowing rice, planting a garden, making friends, I thought little about the windfall due me until shortly before one of our monthly meetings when Mama Komunte reminded me that my turn was next.

My dilemma resurfaced. I didn't want to take the club members' money, and it still felt like their money to me, even though, by then, I had paid into the club exactly the amount of dues I would receive. But there was nothing I needed for my house, and anyway, in another year, I'd be leaving Mzumbe and would only have to get rid of anything I purchased.

That night, I thought about it. I knew Mama Komunte would never accept my outright refusal of the money. So the next day I approached her in the staff room during the morning tea break with a proposal.

"I'll take the money," I told her. "But then I want to put it in a savings account to keep for the club members so that when they need some money to buy medicine for a child or for some other emergency they can take it from the savings account."

Mama Komunte lit up. "That's a wonderful idea," she said. "Then they will pay back the money to the savings account with interest."

I hadn't thought about interest. I hadn't even thought about paying it back. "Well," I said, "I guess so."

"Yes. That is what we will do. That way, we will have more money later for more women to borrow when they need it."

So Mama Komunte rode the *daladala* (local bus) into Morogoro and deposited the 14th month's dues in the brand-new Mzumbe Women Workers' Club Savings Account. It all worked surprisingly well. During the next few months, several club members borrowed small amounts of money and faithfully paid it back with small amounts of interest.

And that might have been the end of it if an announcement hadn't arrived one day in a packet of correspondence from the Peace Corps office in Dar es Salaam. I took the flyer with me to the next Mzumbe Women Workers' Club meeting.

"The Friends of Tanzania* are offering grant money to women's groups," I announced. "Up to 300,000 shillings. All we have to do is think of a business to start."

Everyone put their minds to it. We talked about it during tea break. We talked about it when we met crossing the school grounds. We talked about it when we saw each other in the market. But nothing seemed practical. The librarian, Mama Macha, already had her hands full frying the *mandazi* (donut-like snack) she sold to students during tea break. Besides teaching chemistry, Mama Kihombo raised chickens and sold their eggs in the market in Morogoro to augment her meager school salary. Our club treasurer kept a family cow and sold milk and yogurt. Mama Komunte stitched and embroidered colorful *antimacassars* (cloth) that she sold for wedding gifts. The school secretary managed the village restaurant. The grant deadline was fast approaching, but each woman, it seemed, already ran a small business in addition to her school job and was heavily burdened with work, chores, and family responsibilities. There was no time for another business.

"I know what we will do," Mama Komunte proclaimed at the next club meeting. "We will do what Mama Karen has taught us."

I was startled, unable to imagine what that could be.

---

* *Returned Peace Corps Volunteers often join or form a "Friends of..." group for their country of service. These groups stay involved with country projects both abroad and in the States.*

"Our business will be a credit union," Mama Komunte continued. "We will put the money we receive from this grant from the Friends of Tanzania in our savings account. With that money we can build up our businesses. For instance, one day when Mama Kihombo wants a new chicken house, she can borrow money from our credit union to buy the materials. Then she will have more chickens and more money from the eggs she sells, and she will pay the money back with interest. Our credit union will get bigger and bigger as our businesses get bigger and bigger."

For several afternoons, Mama Komunte and Mama Kihombo huddled in the staff room and wrote the grant. When it was finished, they handed it to me to proofread and mail off to Friends of Tanzania, in time, we hoped, to meet the deadline. Two weeks before my departure from Mzumbe, we received word. Our proposal had been funded.

The last I heard the credit union was going strong. In a letter from Mama Komunte, I learned that, with their growing funds, the Mzumbe Women Workers' Club had broken ground on a new preschool for the village children. They named it, she told me, Karen Kindergarten.

Karen Schaefer served as a secondary school mathematics teacher in Tanzania from 1996-1998. She joined the Peace Corps following a career as a high school mathematics teacher. She and Mama Komunte are now seeking ways to improve maternal healthcare in the village of Mzumbe.

~~~

FINDING MEANING IN HAIR

Andrei Cotton · Ecuador

Yesterday, it happened. As I was elbow-deep in a field of hair in an Ecuadorian orphanage, a truth was revealed to me. Although the revelation happened yesterday, the story began 18 months ago when I traded my comfortable job for a life of adventure and service as a Peace Corps Volunteer in Ecuador.

I began my service as an agribusiness Volunteer. After three months of training in Tumbaco, I moved to my first site, Alor. Alor is a very small community (it seemed to have only about 100 residents) in northern Ecuador situated high in the Andes mountain range. It was a quiet, picturesque community of small farmers. The farmers I worked with jointly owned an integrated farm that produced corn, alfalfa, onion, and guinea pigs. My project was to help them more efficiently manage the farm and find markets for their products. I also helped a local foundation that operated a community bank and provided micro-loans to enterprising families. The project went very well, and after seven months, I left Alor and moved to Las Villegas to work on a larger project.

Las Villegas is a coastal community of approximately 7,000 people. I worked with an association of farmers growing abaca (the fiber from the abaca plant is used to make durable paper products like money, tea bags, and coffee filters). I helped the association members find alternative export markets for their product. After about a year of working, we had joined the newly created National Federation of Abaca Growers, and the Ecuadorian government initiated a feasibility study to build a major abaca processing factory.

Like most Volunteers, I'm also involved in secondary projects when time and opportunity permit. And it was while I was participating in a secondary project that it happened.

Of the 160 Peace Corps Volunteers in Ecuador, seven of us are African American. At the request of a Volunteer working at a girls' orphanage in the capital city of Quito, we visited her place of work to introduce the children to some of the cultural diversity in the United States. We arrived at the orphanage at dusk on a cool, overcast day. We were nervous because it was our first project together. However, as Peace Corps Volunteers we were accustomed to entering the unknown with anticipation and optimism. (There is a Peace Corps saying: A pessimist sees the glass as half empty, an optimist sees the glass as half full, and a Peace Corps Volunteer sees the glass and says, "Hey, I can take a bath in that!").

When we entered the orphanage, we were greeted by a roomful of 25 active children and the nuns who were their caretakers. Most of the children were mestizo and ranged in ages from 5 to 14. Just nine of the children were black. There are few blacks in Quito (most Afro-Ecuadorians live in the coastal province of Esmeraldas), and discrimination against black and indigenous people is, unfortunately, common. These girls were having a difficult time because they were removed from their culture, and they struggled with their sense of worth.

Though these girls seemed to be glad to see us, they also appeared a bit apprehensive and maybe a little ashamed that their hair was in such disarray. Although the children's caretakers did a great job with their limited resources, they simply did not know how to care for the hair and skin of black children.

After making our introductions, we split into two teams. One group of Volunteers entertained the non-black children with games. The other group taught the black children and their caretakers the art of maintaining black hair. Judging from the varying states of disarray of the heads before us, we were going to have our hands full—literally.

We began by talking about self-esteem. We told them how beautiful and important they were and that we would help them to take care of their hair and skin, thus encouraging them to take pride in themselves. Then we gave them a lesson on using ordinary household goods like eggs, oil, aloe, and bananas to care for their hair and skin. Finally, we went to work combing, greasing, and braiding. As we practiced the ancient ritual of the laying on of the hands with a comb in one hand, some grease in the other, and a child between our knees, the conversation revolved around geography, life, and the stack of *Essence, Ebony,* and *Emerge* magazines we had brought with us. Initially, the girls were very shy and saw us as being different from them. But by the end of the night, they realized that we were all the same and began to tell their stories, ask questions, and play with our hair.

And that's when it happened. At some point in the evening, the room had transformed itself. Time, place, language, and nationality fell away and became meaningless. Our kinship and love was conveyed by the texture of healthy hair, the glow of oiled black skin, the smiles of everyone enjoying this moment of connection, and the wonder in the eyes of a child discovering her beauty. By the end of the night, we were all changed, and our bond as a people was solidified. Being "black," or more accurately, "a child of Africa," does not mean that we must speak the same language, act the same way, have similar beliefs, or live in a certain neighborhood, city, or country. We realized that our strength lay in our diversity and barriers could come down with simple affirmations and the combing of hair.

Andrei Cotton served as an agricultural business Volunteer in Ecuador from 1998-2000. Upon completion of his service, he married a fellow Volunteer (Kelly Griffin) and resumed his career in the agribusiness industry. He is now employed as a foreign service officer with the U.S. Department of State.

ANGEL

Barbara Arrington · South Africa

I awoke to the sounds of singing and the pounding of feet. The beautiful yet haunting sound of voices in harmony moved closer as men and women paraded down the red dirt road in a Saturday ceremony for the dead. AIDS was making its own inexorable march across my village of over 3,000 families, snatching someone away almost weekly. And while AIDS was talked about, few people accepted its existence among them. Those who had the disease were shunned.

One of those was a young woman who called herself Angel. When she was born, her mother named her Mankhu, which means death in Northern Sotho. In the end, she would use her life to be an example so that others could live.

My primary job as a Peace Corps Volunteer was to help teachers implement a new outcome-based curriculum adopted by the South African government in their schools. My secondary job was left up to me. Based on the needs of my community, I could decide what project outside of the school I wanted to do. As I sought for the perfect fit, one came knocking at my door.

"Mabatu!" My host mother called out my South African name.

"Yebo, Ke etla!" (Yes, I'm coming!) I replied.

"You have a visitor," my host mother said at my door, coming to me instead.

Outside, under a large mango tree, sat a woman, neatly dressed in a white button-down blouse and navy blue skirt.

"Dumelang" (hello) I said.

"Aowa! O bolela!" (No way! You are speaking my language!) she said as many do when they hear me speak.

Though I am black like they are, I am still a stranger and so they are surprised that I can speak their language. We chatted a while about general, small topics, and then she explained that she had started a home-based care group that would visit the sick in the village and take medicine or food to them. She wondered if I could come and train them about HIV/AIDS and how it is transmitted. I quickly agreed and made arrangements to run a series of weekly workshops at the small village clinic.

Among the regular attendees at these sessions was a young woman in her 20s who sat quietly, listening intently. She was exceptionally thin for her height and walked with a slight limp. I noted her and wondered about her, but never approached her. During a special session, I invited a fellow Volunteer who was a retired nurse to make a presentation. When she was finished and final words were being spoken, the young woman stood up. She thanked me and her smile and beautiful large eyes spoke volumes across cultures, across language barriers. Afterwards, she asked if I could come and visit her. This was the beginning of a significant life lesson for me.

I went the following week to her home. She lived in a small, bare concrete house. Only one of the rooms had walls on all sides. Instead of inviting me in, we sat outside on two wire chairs, and she began to tell me her life story. She didn't know her father, and her mother had left her with her grandmother when she was a girl. She had three children, two of whom lived with relatives. I had often seen her third child in the village. Her current boyfriend, she told me, had given her AIDS. As she continued to talk, I inwardly despaired at the bleakness of her situation. I was there to help, but nothing could prepare me for this woman's story. Nothing could prepare me for the hopelessness or help-lessness I felt. She had no job, no money, and a child to feed. There was no medication for her disease. She had full-blown AIDS and would undoubtedly die within five years.

"Mabatu," she said, "I want to talk to people about my life. I want to warn other girls. You taught me so much. And you didn't just teach; you hugged me. No one ever hugs me because they are afraid they will catch AIDS. Thank you, Mabatu."

She wanted to share her story. I sat stunned, awed that she wanted to talk about her disease to people in a village where she could easily become ostracized. And I was amazed that something so small as my simple hug could mean so much.

I went to the local high schools and middle schools to ask if Angel could come and talk to the life skills classes.

Though the teachers were hesitant, they knew a growing number of teenagers were dying of AIDS and so they agreed that she could speak to the students.

By telling her story, Angel found confidence and a reason to live. She found a church and became part of a community. The challenges were still there, of course. Even my host mother would whisper and ask me why I bothered with such a woman. Yet, she realized, like so many others in my community, that Angel was worthy of being loved, she was worthy of *ubuntu*, which means treating fellow humans with dignity.

Toward the end of my service, Angel asked me to help her make a memory box for her daughters. As we sat together and prepared this box that would be given to her children after her death, I realized she was creating it not with sorrow, but with practicality and love.

I had started out the teacher, but in the end it was I who was taught. She taught me strength and survival and love. She taught me how to live. I often complained about the small worries of life. Now, even so far away from Africa, I remember Angel who learned to embrace her situation, prepare for it, and worked to help others along the way. She taught me that my problems are not so big that they cannot be conquered with courage. Angel still lives as far as I know, and I hope that the memories she has to give to her daughters—through the box she made and how she lived her life—will be many and unforgettable. Like Angel.

Barbara Arrington served as a Peace Corps Volunteer in South Africa from 2002-2004. She worked as a school and community resource Volunteer in a rural village in the province of Mpumalanga. One of her several community projects was working as an HIV/AIDS trainer to a home-based care group. She now works as a volunteer coordinator with Habitat for Humanity.

WHEN THE STUDENT IS READY, THE TEACHER WILL APPEAR

Bernadette Zayas Lorenzo · Paraguay

"When the student is ready, the teacher will appear," the old saying goes. As I slept fitfully underneath my sleeping bag, I awoke to the sounds of thunder, bright lightning, and rain that was soaking Barrio San Josè, the community in Paraguay where I was serving as a Volunteer from 1996 to 1998. Finally, it was 8:00 a.m. and time to wake up. My purpose for the day was to teach a group of mothers in my community how to make *suero oral*. This was a rehydration drink used to treat dehydration caused by anything from sunstroke to diarrhea. Dehydration results when the body loses more fluids than it takes in. It can happen with severe diarrhea, especially when there is vomiting as well. It can also happen when a person is seriously ill, too sick to take much food or liquid. Dehydration develops more quickly and is most dangerous in small children. The rehydration drink replaces crucial fluids and electrolytes lost due to diarrhea, vomiting, and other illness. Teaching the mothers how to make suero oral would make a difference.

When the student is ready, the teacher will appear. As a rural health educator, my job was not only to understand my community and encourage people to adopt behaviors that promoted health and prevent illness, but also to understand the cultural views and socio-political context in which they operated. After having been in Paraguay for 15 months, I realized that the rain meant everything would come to a halt. In the Paraguayan countryside, when it rains, it pours, and everything comes to a standstill. This was especially true in the *campo* (countryside) where the roads turned into muddy rivers and public transportation became non-existent. There would be no buses today to take the people into the neighboring town of Mallorquin where most did their grocery shopping. Community meetings and school classes would be cancelled. The red dirt road in front of my thatched-roofed house became impassable.

When the student is ready, the teacher will appear. I knew that no one would show up at my meeting. I did not even try to go out of my house, and I resigned myself to drinking *maté* (traditional Paraguayan tea) all afternoon long. Still, I was determined to make a difference. I thought to myself if only I could teach one person to make suero oral, the rehydration drink, that could make a difference.

When the student is ready, the teacher will appear. The student came in the form of a 10-year-old boy: my neighbor, Rigoberto, walking his bicycle in the pouring rain as he passed by my house. "Bernie! Bernie!" he called out to me. "Can I come inside your house?" Rigoberto asked.

"*Ndaipori problema,* come on in!" I answered. As he came inside my house, I had my Aha! moment. I could, at least, teach Rigoberto how to make suero oral. I sat him down on my old rickety wooden chair and proceeded to teach him in my not-so-fluent Guaraní and Spanish. (Guaraní is the indigenous language of the Paraguayans, spoken in the campo; Spanish is the official language of Paraguay.) I explained what dehydration was, its symptoms, and how important it was to replace the fluids and electrolytes that the body loses because of diarrhea, vomiting, or other illness.

When the student is ready, the teacher will appear. For 15 minutes, I instructed Rigoberto on how to make suero oral. "OK, Rigoberto," I told him. "We will need 1 liter of boiled and cooled water; 8 teaspoons of sugar; 1 teaspoon of fine, iodized salt; and the juice from 1 lemon. Mix all of these together until all granules have dissolved," I continued. "Place in a clean, covered container and get the child to take in as much as possible." (Coincidentally, the numbers in the ingredients—1811—were also the year Paraguay gained its independence from Spain, so that became a mnemonic for Rigoberto to remember how to make suero oral.) After the rain stopped, our lesson over, he went on his merry way.

When the student is ready, the teacher will appear. Two weeks later, Rigoberto's mother, Doña Carmen, approached me as I passed by her house. She told me how her 10-month-old baby had been sick with severe diarrhea and how Rigoberto had taught her to make suero oral so the baby wouldn't get dehydrated. I was ecstatic!

Though I hadn't been able to teach that group of mothers that rainy afternoon as I'd intended and hoped, I had been able to teach someone, and that had made a difference. Opportunities to teach—and to make a difference—can come in many ways, as Rigoberto showed me that rainy afternoon in Paraguay.

Bernadette Zayas Lorenzo served as a rural health extension Volunteer in Paraguay from 1996-1998. She earned a master of arts degree in political science through the Peace Corps Fellows/USA Program at Illinois State University in 2001. She currently works as a Peace Corps regional recruiter in Atlanta, Georgia.

TALKING OF TREES

Aaron Welch · Dominican Republic

I had never cut down a tree before coming to the Dominican Republic as a Peace Corps Volunteer. Fresh out of training, I understood my job to be simple: I was going to plant trees. Then why did I find myself, in my first weeks in the village, hacking away at sturdy Caribbean pines on the slopes above the village where I was to spend the next two years?

When I spoke of deforestation, villagers told me, "We have trees," and they would point to the ridge tops. They were right; many pine trees did grow on the hills and ridges around the village, clumped here and there between fallow fields of waist-high grass and steep, brown slopes of plowed earth opened up for beans and other cash crops.

"But trees are life," I would protest. This was the slogan of a ubiquitous nonprofit in the region, and a phrase I could easily repeat in Spanish.

"Yes, it's very important," the villagers would agree with me.

Months later I would come to understand the Dominican, "It's very important," meant the same as a slowly muttered "uh-huh" at home. I became frustrated when I heard it, and recognized that it signaled reaching a dead end.

But I didn't know this at the beginning, so I hiked into the hills with a group of men from the village and cut down pine trees that had been damaged in a hurricane two years before. The damage wasn't always obvious, and I felt uneasy about felling trees, especially considering I had been sent to the village to plant more. But I consoled myself with the knowledge that the outing at least provided an opportunity to talk about trees.

In fact, I took every opportunity I could to talk of trees in those early days; of how the hurricane had done away with nearly all the large, old trees along the river; the necessity of trees to the hydrologic cycle; the benefits of trees on the farm, for soil conservation, shade, and as wind breaks. And always I was told, "It's very important." But never in those first months did I manage to inspire any of the villagers to work with me to plant any. Gradually, I spoke less of trees. I became bored with my well-rehearsed entreaties. My Spanish improved, and I found, much to everyone's enjoyment, that I could talk of other things. I began to attend to the daily business of living in a Dominican village.

I made regular visits to the many colorfully painted homes scattered up and down the narrow valley. Mostly, this meant sipping strong coffee, freshly brewed the moment a visitor was seen coming up the path. Sometimes there was much conversation; other times I simply sat and enjoyed the cool breeze blowing through the mountain village. Always, my hosts served the coffee in a tiny cup atop a saucer. To be given a saucer was a sign of respect in a village where there are not enough saucers to go around. I appreciated the gesture and made sure that I held onto the saucer, keeping my cup on it between sips.

I learned to linger in the village stores, or *colmaldos*, where women buy the rice and beans for the day's lunch and other supplies. Occasionally, I would share a Fanta with someone in the colmaldo that day—there were always two or three people passing time at the counter or on the bench under the shade outside. Two stores became my regular hangouts, and visiting them helped shape what became my daily routine. My visits came to be expected, and I enjoyed my newfound place in the community.

Each day, when I returned from my visits, I entertained a gaggle of *muchachos* (boys) on the tiny cement porch at the front of my faded, pink house. I was popular for the tin can of crayons and sheets of scrap paper I kept inside. We bathed in the river on hot afternoons and played games on the patch of dry earth behind my house. If I needed a packet of coffee or an egg to go with lunch, I could always send one of the children to the colmaldo with a peso or two, enough to get whatever I needed and a hard candy for the muchacho.

One afternoon, at a meeting of the village women's group, the topic of trees came up. I had been helping the women to expand a vegetable garden, and we were discussing new seeds they might plant. I heard a voice in the room say something about fruit trees, and I remembered the original reason for my coming. I promised the women we would have fruit trees. I didn't know how we would make this happen, but a renewed sense of purpose rushed over me, and I decided to worry about the details later.

The details proved to be many, and my second year in the village was consumed by attending to each one. The women and I had resolved to create a tree nursery in the village; a site had to be selected, a fence erected, weeds cleared, and tools and materials had to be found. Most difficult of all, we needed support from the rest of the village. But, unlike my first months, now I wasn't the only one talking about trees. This time there were 24 women speaking about trees louder—and more fluently—than me.

The women organized workdays in the tree nursery. As the project grew, I found myself working nearly every day on the parcel of land we had selected. Then the women began to schedule staggered workdays so that at least one or two of them would be there to help me. They used their considerable leverage to get the men in the village to help build the nursery and a neighboring shed to house the tools and shelter the truckload of dark topsoil the government had donated. Slowly, a tree nursery started to take shape.

Now, when I made visits to my friends' colorful homes, or shared a Fanta at the colmaldo, people were talking to me about trees. Even the muchachos were excited. They used my tin can of crayons to draw me pictures of trees we were growing. I shared their excitement, and when the nursery was fully functional, I decided it was time to hang the large sign I had secretly made. The sign named the nursery after the women's group. The women gathered, and we admired the results of our work.

"We have trees," the women declared.

They were right. The tree nursery was half filled with saplings organized neatly into rows of black plastic bags full of dark soil. The sandy germination beds were planted with seeds of a dozen different species. Trees would be planted in the village in a few months' time. Together, we had created something that had the potential to grow and benefit the entire community and the land the community depends upon.

"It's very important," I said with a smile.

Aaron Welch served as an agroforestry Volunteer in the Dominican Republic from 2000-2002. He holds a master's degree in environmental science from Yale University where he was the recipient of the School of Forestry and Environmental Studies' Returned Peace Corps Volunteer scholarship.

~~~~~~~~~

THE FACES OF AN ACACIA TREE

Karin Vermilye · Cameroon

The Cameroonian sky was threatening as the dark rumbling clouds shifted their way quickly toward us, and the kids finished patting down the earth around the last tree. Together, that day in June 2002, we planted 30 trees. It was a small amount in the face of so much sand and nutrient-hungry soil, but a step. A slight breeze was blowing that soothed the prickle of salt on my sweaty skin. Little pieces of paper, with their French and mathematical equations, fluttered past in the savanna grass. I remember squatting next to the last tree we had planted, watching as the students and the teachers gathered up the hoes and shovels. I remember feeling the tiny, delicate, light green leaves with my fingers, and I remember how I saw so many people's efforts within that skinny, young acacia tree.

The Seeds

Alphonse gave us the acacia seeds in November. We had been working with him to develop his small tree nursery into a commercial tree business. We helped him to for-mulate a business plan by scratching figures into the sand in his yard with a small stick. We were calculating how much money he could make, if he grew and sold such-and-such amount of trees, for this-and-that amount of money. That day in November, we told him about the tree nursery at the school.

"Wait," he exclaimed and ran into his hut. He came out with an old, yellow, rusted powdered milk can. He took the plastic lid slowly off the top and told me to hold out my hands. I watched as he poured the slick, brown, shiny seeds from the metal can into my cupped palms. They were small seeds; three could fit on my thumbnail. "These will help," he said. "They are from a strong tree." I wrapped the seeds into a corner of my red bandanna, and put them deep into my pocket.

The Soil

My friend Hapsatou told us where the good soil might be. "Behind the old school," she said. "I have heard it is good there." *"La bonne terre,"* Hapsatou had said. The good earth. Ah, my friend Hapsatou. Almost every night for the two years we lived in Touroua, we ate dinner with her and her family. Over pounded millet and green-leaf sauc-es, perhaps with a side of bony fish, we would discuss our days. As my French improved, I worked at describing all the details of what had happened that day. We would tell her who we had seen, what they had said, and how all the trees in the nurseries scattered around the village were growing. She was so eager for contact and for information.

Hapsatou was a married Muslim woman in a very traditional area. Our village in the north of Cameroon practiced wife seclusion. This means that once a woman is married, she does not often leave her home. There are some exceptions. She can venture from her compound walls if one of her children is sick so she can go to the clinic or the *marabou*. She can also leave to attend a wedding or a funeral or if one of her friends is sick or giving birth. With this practice, the children become the women's messengers, running from house to house exchanging the news and gossip.

In the first few months that I was there, my stomach often revolted against the new foods and the heat that were so foreign to me. Hapsatou's five-year-old son El Kass would come to visit us, and see me lying in the hammock or outside the doorway on a mat.

"*Jabamma, El Kass,*" I would say. Welcome.

"*Jam na, Kareen?*" he would ask me in the traditional Fulfulde greeting that meant literally, "do you have peace?"

"*Jam ne, El Kass.*" It's all good.

"*Jam bandu na?*" How's your body?

"*Na boddum, sobajo am.*" Not good, my friend.

At this, El Kass would turn and run home, without even bothering to finish the traditional string of greetings, including how's the work, how's your house, how are your goats, how are the fields, and how's the heat (which would always make him giggle). He would tell Hapsatou that I was, once again, *mal au ventre.*

This made me a source of freedom for her. She would come over as soon as she heard I wasn't feeling well, bringing with her a bowl of thick and sweetened *bouille*. The thick, milky porridge was usually slightly flavored with lemons and was a wonderful combination of sweet and sour. I would lie on the mat sipping the bouille while she sat next to me. She would talk about the plants she thought I should know, and tell me who was good to work with in the village and who to avoid.

The first time we walked through our village together was on the way to my first funeral. Hapsatou, her husband Abba, my husband Brian, and I had walked into the compound together when we first arrived. Hapsatou motioned me one way as I watched Brian and Abba disappear behind one of the red mud walls.

Then I heard the crying. I peeked inside the hut and saw 35 women, packed shoulder-to-shoulder within the dark interior. Many of the women were steadily and quietly crying while rocking forward and back. Then, one old woman with wrinkled hands reached out to me in greeting, entwined her fingers within mine, opened her mouth, and let out a long and loud wail. The feeling was surreal, surrounded by weeping women in a wailing hut in Cameroon, but Hapsatou's eyes caught mine, and she steadied me.

My friend Hapsatou, who had wrapped me so well within her nourishment, had given us directions to the most productive soil in town, even though she could not walk there herself.

The Water

Abduli was dressed in his long, pale, brown robe that reached to his knees with the matching pants below. The sweat was beading on his forehead and rolling down onto his lips. He blew the droplets off his pursed lips, and concentrated on flipping the black rubber bucket just right so it would fill quickly. When he was satisfied and felt the tug of the right weight of water on the rope, he pulled the bucket hand-over-hand back to the surface. He poured the water into the silver metal bucket sitting in a puddle by the well. He did this several times until the water lapped at the rim of the metal bucket.

Then, he carefully started to lift the bucket to his head. His friend Amadou spotted him and came to help lift the heavy load. Together, they placed the sloshing container on Abduli's head, and did not spill but a few drops. Abduli slowly walked to the corner of the yard where the tree nursery was, and filled the watering cans. The watering cans were old plastic containers with holes punched in the top, but they worked acceptably. He made two more trips to the well and back to make sure all the seedlings were watered. Then he washed his hands and head and finally took a long drink from the well.

So many hands were involved in giving life to that acacia tree. It came to exist through the effort of the community, and the interest of individuals. In a few years, that tree will become tall and thorny, with a dense flat crown and dark fissured bark. Each of its branches will tell the story of the man who gathered the seeds, the woman who knew where the good soil was, the students who pulled the water from the well, and all the others who worked to plant green trees on the dusty land.

Karin Vermilye worked as a forestry extension agent while a Peace Corps Volunteer. She and her husband, Brian App, served in Cameroon in the Sahel Agroforestry Program from 2000-2002. Karin was a participant in Peace Corps' Master's International program through the University of Montana, and earned a master's in resource conservation in May 2004.

~

WOMEN CAN LEARN THINGS TOO

Amber B. Davis-Collins · Honduras

Cerro Grande was a two-hour walk up the mountain from my town of San Pedro de Tutule. The dirt road ended abruptly about a mile before arrival—a government project gone awry. Instead, patrons of this little community at the top of the mountain (population 110) had two choices—a steep, slick trail that took about 20 minutes from the dirt road, or a more gentle approach that took twice as long. I always chose the latter, which ended near Don José and Doña Maria's house.

I originally met Don José at a baby weighing in Granadillo. This is a community event where mothers bring their children to be weighed so that adequate nutrition and healthy development can be tracked. I was about three-fourths of the way through my Peace Corps service at the time. He had heard that the *gringa* in Tutule had vegetable seeds and wanted some for his family. He was the only man in attendance at the baby weighing that day. In fact, Don José was the only man that I ever saw at a baby weighing during my two years in Honduras. He didn't speak until every child had been weighed and most of the women had taken their children and returned home.

"They tell me that you have seeds," he said, not looking at my face.

"Yes," I answered. "But today I have only carrots." I handed him a packet.

"Do you want me to come to your house and help when you plant?" I asked, hoping that I hadn't offended him.

"Yes, please," he whispered. "I live in Cerro Grande," he said, pointing to the top of the mountain. And so our friendship began.

On my first visit two days later, none of his six children spoke to me. Five of them stood behind their mother, Doña Maria, while Don José made introductions. The other, still too young to walk, stayed in Doña Maria's arms and wailed. Doña Maria appeared sullen and withdrawn. The two-room house was made of rocks, sticks, and mud. A ragged dog tended to its scraggly pup next to the earthen stove.

The kids giggled and ducked their faces when I directed my small talk toward them, but none mustered up the courage to reply. "They have never seen a white person before," said Doña Maria flatly, as if this explained everything. And I guess it did. In an area of the world that still didn't have electricity, much less radios or televisions, my blond hair, blue eyes, and pale skin must have been quite a spectacle.

All the children except the youngest came out to watch Don José and me plant the garden that afternoon. A few of the neighbors came, too. We were obviously the biggest entertainment venue in town that day. As we worked, I asked about the school that I had passed on my way up the mountain. "The teacher almost never comes," Don José explained. "It's been too rainy and the walk is just too long."

"That's terrible!" I exclaimed.

Don José shrugged his shoulders. "The boys aren't old enough for school yet."

I looked over at the two oldest children, both girls, standing shyly at the edge of the garden. "What about the girls?" I asked.

Don José laughed. "They have work to do."

As I pressed on, Don José revealed that his wife had never gone to school and that he himself had only gone for two years. That's all that he was going to require of his sons, too, provided that the school ever got a regular teacher. "But there's no one in Cerro Grande that can teach," he added softly.

Over the next few months, I trekked up the mountain every week or so to check on the garden, as well as to visit Don José and his family. More often than not, Don José was away, and I would end up passing the time with Doña Maria and the children instead. I brought more seeds—onions, sweet peppers, and radishes. We talked a lot about gardening—the importance of thinning and weeding, how often to water, and how a diversified diet would make her family healthier (their nutritional regime at the time consisted of corn, beans, and an occasional bit of rice). She and the children worked in the garden with me when I visited, but most of the work was done when I wasn't around. It wasn't long before shoots started springing up.

As time went by, this woman that I had once dreaded visiting because she seemed so bitter, began to open up. We talked about her family and her life before she married José. Doña Maria's past had not been rich with opportunity. Although she never said it, and probably didn't even realize it, I could tell that a difficult life had left her emotionally numb. But things were changing—she began to smile and talk excitedly each time I arrived at the house. She greeted me with an ear of corn and laughed when I played with the kids. There was a definite transformation in the house of Don José and Doña Maria.

On one of my last trips up the mountain before I completed my service, Don José was home. I began my visit with the obligatory soccer match with the children. (The ball was an ancient wadded-up plastic bag tied into a ball shape with a piece of string.) Afterwards, the entire family moved out to the garden to admire the work that everyone had done over the last few months.

Standing in the garden, Don José pulled a mature carrot out of the ground. "You know," he said thoughtfully, "I'm really glad that you have been helping Maria. Because of you, I have realized that women can learn things too."

My first reaction as an educated woman was to laugh because I was sure that he was joking. But when I looked at his face, I saw that he was serious. And the stark realization for me was that this was a totally new insight for Don José. After I was able to close my gaping jaw, I met his smile with one of my own. In the background I could hear Doña Maria laughing.

Amber B. Davis Collins served as a crop extensionist Volunteer in Honduras from 2002–2004. She has a master's degree in agricultural education from the University of Georgia. Amber currently works in the pesticides program of the U.S. Environmental Protection Agency in Atlanta and was recently awarded a bronze medal by the agency for her work with Latino farm worker issues.

THE WORK CONTINUES

Kelly Daniel · Kenya

Her name is Irene and her breath comes in ragged blasts, like the sound of an old bicycle pump pushing air as best it can. Her family waits for that sound to fall silent. It will not be long.

The day before I stand in Irene's house, so deep into the bush that the women I'm with point out crushed branches and limbs, saying, "Elephant," I stand in front of bored high school students, kept a day beyond school's closing by a paperwork snafu. I run through my bag of tricks, barren, as it must be after only 10 weeks of trying to teach HIV/AIDS prevention, close the session, and field questions from a few students interested or scared enough to stay behind. A sharp-eyed teen named Diana looks me over. "These people who have AIDS, what do you do for them?" she asks. Words tumble from my mouth, a jumble of platitudes. Diana cuts into my ramble. "But what do you *do* for them?" "I try," I answer at last.

Irene lies on a double bed that allows no other furniture into the room that holds her, her mother, eight of my companions, and me. I am with an AIDS group newly trained in home-based care for patients across our 10 villages. This is our first visit. All I know of our patient before we arrive is that she is terribly sick. She is more than that. The jovial mood of the eight good friends on the hike to this tiny house has vanished; grim, but not horrified expressions are on every face. I look around the *manyatta*—the circular huts of mud-stick-grass splayed across so much of Africa—and listen to the rasps coming from the bed. Diana's question swims in my head.

Irene is caught in a state of "not." Not really living; not quite dead. She no longer moves, sees, hears. She feels pain, heard in the wretched whimpers echoing from the bed when two of our group bathe her. I know almost nothing about her, save her name, what is killing her, and where she will die. I do not know her age, but guess that she is no more than in her early 30s. My age.

Her father sits outside with a younger man (perhaps her husband?) and three children, at least one of which is hers. I do know that she is loved. Her mother, her own long life evidenced in a leathery face and wisps of grey hair visible beneath her head wrap, moves from the head of the bed to the foot, to the door frame and back, never out of sight. She does not speak to her daughter while we are there, but her hands are always reaching out. Her fingers peck at the blankets, rearranging them and re-rearranging, constantly.

Her hands know they do not have much longer to touch this life they held first, and most often. I sit and watch.

The group believes I know more than they do about providing care for AIDS patients. I do not, and have not been able to get them to understand this. They will turn to me for guidance and reassurance throughout the day.

Luckily, there is a single moment when I do know what needs to be done, having somehow picked up knowledge over the years of the proper way to turn a bedridden patient. I stand at the footboard as Alice, tall and regal, feeds Irene *uji*, a porridge/millet mixture. Lydia, squat, plump, funny, is at Alice's elbow, swatting blasted flies that are taking advantage of the fact that Irene's eyes are perpetually half opened, her mouth in the same repose. The mother stands at the headboard, fingers cupping Irene's small head, raising it slightly for the waiting spoon. A sound like a blocked drain unclogging is the only cue that Irene has swallowed the food, and Alice delivers another spoonful. Lydia has the look of someone who wishes she had something more substantial to do. I know that look. I stand and watch these four women and am filled with such a sense of love, of blessing, that I nearly explode into tears. Later, the anger will come: how unnecessary, this disease, these losses! The slender, gentle sets of fingers gripping the spoon, the head, the blanket, the air where a fly was; those are what affect me and what I remember.

Most of my time these last few weeks has been spent at the opposite end of the spectrum, with schoolchildren who mostly do not have HIV/AIDS. And we want to keep it that way. I've taught 11 basic HIV lessons in seven schools so far. I'm quicker on my feet than I've any right to be—given the shortness of time in this role—in fielding questions from kids, many of whom want nothing more than to embarrass the *mzungu* who has come to talk to them about sex, death, life, and disease. It's impossible to be self-conscious in these moments, so absurd are the scenarios, so surreal the situations.

AIDS in Kiswahili, by the way, is *Ukimwi*. I've yet to find someone who can translate "HIV." So many Kiswahili words are borrowed from the Arabic, Portuguese, and English conquerors of East Africa in millennia past that some phrases have no alternate and the Kiswahili speaker just stands, blinking, when I ask how to say something like avocado in the language. "Avocado," he or she answers. Oh.

My eight companions and I ride back to Ndome, having hiked more kilometers than I know that morning. The women sing the buoyant, joyous songs all Kenyan women sing en route somewhere, even if it is just from the kitchen to the sitting room. Our packed little posse bounces along the dirt, a parade of song, as the driver turns up the road to my dispensary. I sit there, remembering in that moment the rise and fall of the green blanket across Irene's miserable chest, and I look at the smiling faces of the women I am with and their happiness at a long walk deferred. Extreme highs, extreme lows, dozens of them packed into each day. Always, among the saddest moments, a reminder of the joys that fill this world. I feel blessed for the ability to take it all in.

Irene died the next day. The work continues.

Kelly Daniel served as a public health Volunteer in Kenya from 2003-2005. She joined the Peace Corps after a career in newspaper journalism.

~

NOT A WASTE OF TIME AT ALL

Ronald Venezia · Guatemala

We arrived in San Juan Comalapa, Guatemala, in
1963 in the back of an open jeep—Bonny, Jim, and me—a
young man from suburban New York City. Caked with
dust from the dirt road, we were part of the first group of
Peace Corps Volunteers to live in the Guatemalan highlands. Three months of training had given us some Spanish, a general knowledge of cooperatives, and an appetite
for adventure. We settled into an old adobe *pensión*, con-
verting it into a community center. For the next 18 months,
we worked in this small village—Comalapa had 6,000 people and 90 percent of them were Mayan Indians. Bonny
worked in home economics, Jim was assigned to agriculture, and I was tasked with forming a credit cooperative.

Comalapa sat nestled in a high plain against a set of low
mountains. It was cut off from easy access to a highway 16
kilometers away by a forbiddingly deep ravine traversed
by a narrow dirt road with wicked switchbacks down and
up its length. Despite its relative isolation, however, the

village population had a reputation of being hard-working farmers and active traders in the region's markets. Electricity was available in the town's urban area, but communication was by telegraph and an unreliable postal system. Urban architecture was mostly one-story adobe and tile-roofed structures, pockmarked by alternating painted and faded dirt facades, spreading out from a main square, which was dominated physically and spiritually by a huge colonial church. Socially, traditional *cofradias** were slowly giving way to an emerging evangelical presence, as well as to influences from the modern Catholic Church. Transportation was mainly by buses where passengers would intermingle with animal and produce cargo. Cars were a rare sight. A small group of Indians had started painting primitive scenes of daily life and rites on coffee tin covers to sell that captured the vivid colors of the native handwoven textiles worn by all the women.

I remember our tremendous expectations as we arrived. Imbued by John Kennedy's rhetoric, we thought we were going to do all these great things, convinced we would make history. The cooperative development project was meant to help the isolated mountain villages save money and invest in their own economic growth. Unfortunately, cooperatives had been used for political purposes by previous governments, and there was a deep suspicion about starting a new venture. After six months of seeking out community leaders, and with the help of our Indian counterpart, Santiago Xet, I managed to gather and convince a

* *Indian religious fraternities dating from pre-colonial times*

group of farmers to create the San Juan Comalapa Credit Cooperative. I grandiosely made the inaugural deposit of $5. While I hoped that many more deposits would follow, deep in my gut I feared there was little chance of long-term success. We all then traveled to Guatemala City to register the co-op with the banking authorities. For most of the farmers, this was their first time visiting a government office in the capital.

From that beginning, and with a small grant from USAID, we built a small office building on a donated lot and bought office equipment and a safe. I taught basic accounting. By the end of my service, the co-op had about 50 members, and it was making small loans. I thought this was pretty small potatoes and wrote a piece for the Peace Corps magazine called "A Profitable Waste of Time." In my article, I said that what had been accomplished was not nearly as much as we had expected. I thought that while I had grown personally, Comalapa and its citizens remained largely unaffected.

The next 40 years were not easy on the village of Comalapa. It suffered through a bloody civil war, a devastating earthquake, and uneven harvests. Miles away from the Guatemalan highlands, I had moved on to a successful 30-year career at USAID and then consulting with the World Bank and the U.S. Department of Labor on international development programs—a life-long legacy of my Peace Corps experience. Yet, part of me was still deeply attached to Comalapa and the co-op I'd helped start with five bucks.

In 2003, almost four decades after I arrived as a Peace Corps Volunteer, I returned to Comalapa. I was somewhat apprehensive and didn't know what to expect. Certainly the town would be different: our old home was probably razed in the earthquake, old friends probably would have passed on, and the co-op would probably be out of business.

Driving into town, on a lark, I asked a passing Mayan where the credit co-op was located. I had steeled myself to having my worst expectations realized, musing about what had happened to the small steel safe and simple office equipment we had used in the dirt-floored back room. To my surprise he said, "It's on the main street." Moving down the street, I was dumbstruck to see a brand-new building with a huge electric sign and wide glass doors. Inside, there was a brightly lit lobby with three teller stations, all with computer terminals connected to the Internet. It was everything I had hoped for, but nothing I had expected. The cooperative, much like the town of Comalapa, had weathered many challenges in the past 40 years, but during that time, it had grown steadily in members and funds. The entire staff was made up of educated local Mayan professionals who were delighted to meet the legendary "Don Ron" and learn of the co-op's early beginnings. I almost fell off my chair when I read in the annual report that the co-op had 3,000 members and $900,000 in capital, much of it from remittances from the United States.

Comalapa has changed somewhat, as well. The main road is now paved, the urban streets have paving blocks, a new church has risen next to the severely damaged colonial structure, and a cell tower now rises out of the main square. The nascent primitive painters' community has mushroomed into a local industry with galleries and a private art museum, advertised by a 50-foot-tall billboard at the entrance to town. A popular poster on sale throughout Guatemala depicts the interior of a Comalapa bus in all its variety.

So, the co-op that emerged out of a small Peace Corps project and was founded with my $5 deposit had grown into a major local financial intermediary that offered loans and a variety of savings, mortgages, insurance, and checking services, including receiving remittances from Guatemalans living in the U.S. to their families. For almost 40 years, it has faithfully served the people of Comalapa. It recently opened a branch in the nearby town of Tecpan. I thought to myself, "This is much more than I had always hoped for—maybe we did make some history after all."

In the final analysis, of course, this accomplishment belongs to the village of Comalapa, with its proud and industrious people who knew how to succeed. Forty years of hindsight have also revealed that my work there was indeed profitable and not a waste of time after all.

Ronald Venezia served as a cooperative specialist Volunteer in Guatemala from 1963–1965. He retired from the U.S. Agency for International Development in 1994, as USAID mission director to Costa Rica. Since then, he has consulted with the World Bank on social projects in the former Soviet Union, and most recently with Abt Associates, Inc., on CAFTA-related labor projects in Central America.

LIFE *is* CALLING

"Lessons from our region show that peace must be built between peoples. It derives from understanding, trust, and a sense of working toward a shared destiny. It arises only out of mutual and equitable exchange of skills, of ideas, of cultural values. Peace Corps Volunteers—going where they are invited; bringing open minds, dedication, and enthusiasm; living and working side-by-side with their hosts; and returning with new perspectives to share with those at home—are among the best examples of how that peace will be achieved."

QUEEN NOOR AL HUSSEIN
JORDAN

RENEWABLE RESOURCES: GROWING UP WITH "SARGE" SHRIVER'S BIGGEST FANS

Adrienne Benson Scherger · Nepal

My brother is the black sheep of the family. He married a year out of college and went to law school, which he loved. Soon afterwards he became a lawyer and a father. I admire his rebellious spirit. I, on the other hand, split up with my college boyfriend just before graduation. He went back home to Alaska, and I packed a backpack and headed for the Himalayas to work as a Peace Corps Volunteer in Nepal. I always was the dutiful daughter.

Ever since I can remember, Sargent Shriver's name has been a household word. My parents would often pause in the middle of a story about their Peace Corps experience and sigh, "Good old Sarge Shriver." In Zambia, when I was a small child, my parents were working for the American Friends Service Committee. Those were the days of little extra money, and we used to vacation by taking extended camping trips in our VW van. Driving through the game parks, my brother and I would bounce up and down shriek-ing, "Whoever sees an elephant first gets a brownie!" My mother would turn from her position in the passenger seat to say, "Settle down, you guys. Let me tell you about the time I lived right by the ocean." Nothing would calm me like imagining my mother with her long, black braids setting up a home in a bamboo house, a house on stilts at the edge of a Philippine island.

My father would enrapture us with stories, as well. He'd pause, mid-sentence, to twist up the edges of his handlebar mustache and launch into a story of the Rajasthan desert—narrow escapes from deadly asps or trying to teach Hindu camel herders to raise chickens. He even claimed to have learned to hypnotize chickens in Peace Corps training.

My mother, formerly Pamela Cohelan (Philippines 10), and my father, David Benson (India 5), were both Peace Corps Volunteers. They served under Kennedy, under "Good old Sarge Shriver." Growing up with their stories and their commitment to development work, there was never a time when I didn't dream of joining the Peace Corps myself.

My parents even met one another through the Peace Corps. My mom closed service and embarked on a round-the-world trip. She was headed home to a job at Peace Corps headquarters in Washington, D.C. My father closed service, but stayed on in India by taking a staff position at the northern regional office. During her visit to India, my mother met some Volunteers, one of whom was my fa-ther, and the rest is history. They laid eyes on each other and suddenly a job at Peace Corps headquarters didn't seem quite so appealing. My mother found herself a position with the Peace Corps regional office in Calcutta and six weeks—yes, six weeks!—after they met they were married in a church in Bombay. He sweating in a dark suit; she wrapped in a crimson sari.

When I was accepted to Peace Corps almost 30 years later, my parents were thrilled. When they heard I was going to Nepal, they began planning their trip. I had grown up in Africa, so Asia was a welcome new horizon for me and, of course, a cause for nostalgia for them.

Some things about being a second-generation Peace Corps Volunteer were great. My parents understood my angst-filled, sometimes lonely letters home. They could talk about sustainable development and the frustrations of village life. They laughed with me in recognition of generic Peace Corps stories, pit latrines, and overcrowded buses. My mother and I found solidarity in the classic female Volunteer weight gain and in the multitude of marriage proposals from strange men (my father's proposal to her not included).

As a Volunteer in the 1990s, I was often told that things are much easier for contemporary Volunteers than they were "back in the day." I'm sure that's true in many ways. However, when my parents first made the hike into Pula Bhirmuni, my village under the edge of a cliff in the Kali Gandaki river valley, both of them said that my site, my Peace Corps life, was harder than theirs had been. Of course, much of that assertion had to do with the fact that I am their baby daughter, but I still felt, upon hearing it, that I'd arrived.

The women in the village were so impressed that I had a family. Many hadn't been convinced that I was not simply some unconnected entity, with them because I had nowhere else to be. A young, unmarried woman voluntarily so far away from her family was simply too bizarre to imagine. My mother wore a *shalwar kameez* (a long tunic with baggy pants), which was a huge success. We spent a day down in the rice paddies with the women. The tiny, terraced fields were emerald with the new rice growth and were bordered with golden, blooming soybeans. Amongst the laughter and singing of the women, we tried our best to work the rice. The women shrieked with mirth, "Aasa!" they yelled my village name, "your mother can do this better than you can!"

From Nepal, my parents continued on to India, where they visited my father's old Peace Corps site. Thirty years after his service had ended, they were given a wonderful reception. Everyone still remembered him and his chicken projects.

I hope that there are some people in Pula Bhirmuni who will remember me if I am lucky enough to go back in 30 years. I have two children of my own now whom I hope someday will clamor to hear my Peace Corps stories. Maybe they will even be third-generation Peace Corps Volunteers, children raised on images of their mother making a home for herself in a little stone house in the shadow of the mountains in Nepal.

Adrienne Benson Scherger served as a Peace Corps Volunteer English teacher and teacher trainer in Nepal from 1992–1994. She later worked at Peace Corps headquarters in the Africa region. Besides being a freelance writer and editor, she currently works as the community liaison officer at the U.S. Embassy in Tirana, Albania, where her husband is an administrative officer for the Peace Corps.

HOPE DIES LAST

Patrick Burns · Moldova

I travel because I like to explore, I explore because I like to learn, I learn because I like to understand. It was with these thoughts in mind that I set out for Peace Corps/

Moldova in June 2003. Since then, it has been one lesson after the next.

When I landed in my pre-service training village of Mereseni, it was very quiet, hot, and dusty. I remember thinking to myself that this is where I'll spend the next 10 weeks of my life learning the Romanian language, Moldovan culture, and a lot about myself. My host family was warm, friendly, and very hospitable. This meant that they would offer me their best *vin de casa* (wine of the house) upon my entering through the gate. Immediately, I realized that this was unlike any other wine I'd ever tasted. It was very young and tasted more like fortified grape juice than the wine I was used to drinking in other countries. However, I accepted their generosity and drank a glass. I was able to have a conversation at about a two-year-old level, which was a very humbling experience and reminded me of when I was an exchange student in Mexico during the early 1980s. I knew that the language would come, just how fast and at what speed remained to be seen. Two days later, I had my answer, six hours a day of language training at an amazing pace. What a way to go—and it works!

My fondest memory of the village is a little, seven-year-old girl named Irina. She had a beautiful smile and a curiosity as to what the American was doing in her village. Moreover, she had the patience to practice Romanian with me, a 41-year-old Volunteer. As the summer went on, I started teaching her English words and she'd sit outside the gate and wait for me to get home from school. She always wanted to know what I had learned that day. One day I received a care package from my mother back home and it contained Oreos. I gave Irina a sleeve and she sat there with the biggest smile you could imagine and ate them all. After a while the group got larger, and I was up to seven in this informal learning group. They learned from me, and I learned from them. I learned that, at times, the Peace Corps makes corporate America seem slow; we accomplish more in an hour than some firms do in a week. There are times when we move at light-speed, times when the clock seems to stand still, and times when it appears to run in reverse.

During pre-service training, I was assigned to teach business English during practice school at a local university in the capital of Chisinau. At the end of my three-week course, one of my students came up to me and gave me a kiss on the cheek because she was so excited to practice and improve her English. This was very special because she's an English teacher here in Moldova. Another student brought me a gift from her village. My students were so passionate to learn that it was difficult to understand how Moldova could be so poor. But the next generation has hope. In Moldova, there is a saying, *"Speranta moare ultima!"* (Hope dies last!)

There were times when I'd wonder what sort of an impact the Peace Corps and I were having on Moldova and my students. The best answers I can give are the following examples. First, my wife Rosie and I wanted to travel back home to see our ill fathers as they were both coping with diseases. Upon telling my students that we'd be going to Seattle, two of them asked if they could see us off at the train station. "Of course," I responded. When we met Vadim and Cristina at the train station, they were holding two boxes of local chocolates and two bottles of Moldovan wine.

Cristina said, "These are for your parents. We want to thank them for having you!" I know that those chocolates never tasted better or the wine smoother.

The second example happened during one of my English language club meetings before the Christmas holiday during my first year as a Volunteer. I asked the group to write an answer to the question, "If there was a Santa Claus, what would you want him to bring Moldova?"

One of the students in the group responded, "Freedom, and the knowledge to know how to use it." This remarkable answer led to a discussion of what it means to be free, the rights and responsibilities that we share when we live in a democracy, and the importance of improving ourselves to better our future and our community's future.

I believe that the most important thing we do as Volunteers is provide hope. Everything else seems like an ancillary detail. This sounds so easy doesn't it? That's because we're Americans, and we were born with a sense of optimism that doesn't always exist elsewhere. A British friend once told me that he thinks that Americans have an optimism chip planted in our heads at birth. And so it goes.

To my friends, colleagues, and students in Moldova who helped me understand, *"Multumesc mult!"* (Thank you very much!)

"Speranta moare ultima!"

Patrick Burns served as a Volunteer in Moldova from 2003–2005. He joined the Peace Corps after 18 years as a stockbroker/sales manager. He is currently pursuing a career in the U.S. Department of State as a foreign service officer.

SOYBEAN TRANSFORMATIONS

John Sheffy · Togo

I arrived in Togo in June 2002 with 20 other Peace Corps trainees. Some of us, like myself, were assigned to work in the area of natural resource management and agriculture, and others would be small business development Volunteers. The Peace Corps took the small business Volunteers to their training site, Kpalime, the main regional market city and a paradise of Togolese movers and shakers. Our training group went directly to live with our host families and received an immersion into Togo village life. Suddenly we had no electricity and the only running water was the water your host sister carried from the river and you poured from a cup over your head. Over the next 11 weeks, we attended information sessions on feeding chickens to feeding ourselves; vegetable gardening to garnering understanding of HIV/AIDS; mapping village resources to managing local customs.

After training, I was assigned to Kuma-Dunyo, a highland village of 300 farmers. It was early September, the end of the rainy season, when I arrived. The village awoke before dawn. When I arose at seven, all the compounds were empty, *foyers* (mud stoves) left smoking; it was almost like the villagers had abandoned their camp and moved on. Everyone had already gone to farm during the few good hours of the lifting fog before the sky darkened and the rains began. Armed with my French *dictionnaire de poche* (pocket dictionary), I followed, leaping over rivers of ants on their perpetual search for somewhere higher to hide from getting washed away.

Once at the fields, it became apparent right away that I knew nothing about traditional agriculture. I hand gestured and grunted my way into the ranks of farmers, plunging countless node-covered, red-colored sticks into ridges of red-colored earth. The old man cutting up the branches for us to plant corrected me as I went. My nodes were usually pointed in the wrong direction and the angle I stuck my sticks too steep. In front of my gang of planters were the diggers, overturning the rich top layer of soil by hand with crooked, arm-length hoes. They worked in what seemed like the most awkward body position possible, bent over, shoveling between their legs, like swinging a maul while playing Twister. This was all part of the *manioc* (yam) growing ritual, a means of starch production that sustained the village.

These field visits went on for weeks, every day a revelation of crops, trail systems, and work songs; women, the foundation of all village life, balancing loads of leaves, tubers, and firewood on their heads. They were doing the hardest work with the most stamina I have seen. But, unless measured by blisters and insect bites, my daily tromps didn't seem to be getting me any closer to being an effective Volunteer. Over fogged-in morning silence and the numbing static of evening rain on my aluminum roof, I dreamt of integrated conservation and development projects. I fantasized about calling meetings with the elders, defining the village's needs, facilitating brainstorming sessions, and drawing multicolored flipcharts to match the color of fields. I fantasized about flipcharts; I needed something to do.

My house was in the southwest corner of the village, by the *moulin* (mill) and avocado forest, in one of the village's

five clans. I heard stories that elders of each clan and the chief make up a village development committee. I visited the committee members several times a week asking them when their next meeting would be. The response was always the same: "This week we'll be meeting for sure." But the meetings never came, and gradually I stopped going to the fields. It was November and the dry season's harmattan winds had thrown sand in the sky. During communal labor one morning, when the debris was swept off the public sitting space into the road and burned, the haze blew in a smoky screen. In a few days, the haze seemed like it was always there and would never go away.

At this time, I was grasping the languages and studying the six-inch stack of handouts we were given during training. It took a month to wade through the case studies from past Volunteer projects. It was like someone had run through a library and torn a page out of every book; yet, over time, I organized the papers into chapters. That's how badly I needed to organize something. One chapter was on food preservation and transformation techniques.

Men had pulled my leg enough times with the old "village development meeting" joke while their wives sweated over the cooking fire, that I decided this chapter could be of use. I swept the village; hit all 62 kitchens, telling everyone to meet in the sitting place on *Mercredi* (Wednesday) to learn how to use *soja* (soy). On Tuesday, I rode my bike to town, 30 minutes screaming down the mountains, three hours slugging back up. We didn't have soy in our village market, so I bought the equivalent of $2 worth of dried soybeans, which was a backpack full.

After soaking the beans overnight, I gathered my cooking gear and began making trips to the meeting place to get ready. On my first trip, a few ladies were sitting on the half log benches socializing. They were wrapped in colorful, mismatching *pagne* (printed cloth) costumes like they were going to church or the market. It was obvious something was astir. By the time we started heating the first giant *marmite* (pot) of water, at least 40 women were present. Although I hadn't invited them, there were at least as many men there, too, standing in a circle outside the women as if supervising, but not there to learn. Were villagers that interested in free food?

I quickly recognized that soy had little to do with this meeting. This was about me, my fantasy village meeting, and wild potential scenarios. How would I get everyone to participate? What would the village priorities be? Would there be an elaborate decision-making ceremony between the elders? Was I ready? I had spent the last three days reading all my notes about soy, wondering if using my blue cloth as a filter would make blueberry soymilk, and why in the world I was giving open-fire cooking lessons to village mamas who could reach their bare hands into a boiling pot of water with a smile. I scanned the crowd of eyes looking back at me. They all seemed to be asking the same question, the same question I was asking myself: What is this American doing here? And my response was...soybeans?

As I scribbled my first flipchart notes and the cooking fire battled the smoky, harmattan winds to keep the soy boiling, I began to feel like I was drawing a treasure map for a crew of pirates. But the pirates knew the map all along. The village had not been waiting for me; not looking for someone to organize village meetings or facilitate its development. The people didn't need me to figure out what was wrong.

I was answering Ama's questions about my age and why I wasn't married. I was questioning Madame Comfort's cooking critique, that one must never change their stirring direction. I was trying to explain to Yawa why more sugar doesn't always taste better. At the same time, I was doling out samples of soy couscous to bashful members of the crowd and spouting the values of soy from nutritional, environmental, and economic standpoints. Somehow the people were listening, asking questions, and having a great time.

My role seemed to solidify as the soy milk curdled into cheese. I wasn't starring in the film, *Bringing Soy to the Village*; I was part of an experiment. There wasn't going to be a Volunteer project like digging a well or building a school. As time went by, I learned what was important to people and where they wanted me to intervene. I formed friendships with them that allowed us to discuss realities of problems, not myths about what I should be doing and what they should be wanting. That day, we filtered our soy and ourselves out of the smokescreen and ate our efforts—efforts we tasted over the next two years of experimenting with assumptions and learning as things constantly changed, leaving an aftertaste that lingers on my tongue to this day.

John Sheffy served as a natural resource management Volunteer in Togo from 2002-2004. As a Master's International participant, he conducted the field research for his thesis on participatory forest management in the Ghana-Togo highlands while serving in the Peace Corps. Today, he is applying his Peace Corps experiences in Western Montana.

SAYING GOODBYE

Caroline Chambre · Burkina Faso

It hardly seems possible that two years ago I was watching, more than a little teary-eyed, as the official Peace Corps Land Cruiser pulled away from my new home and headed slowly out of my village. I had heard stories of Volunteers being dropped off in their new homes, only to go quickly chasing after the vehicle exclaiming, "Wait—I'm not ready yet!" I had laughed at those stories at the time, but as the Land Cruiser faded from sight, I felt a kinship with those fabled Volunteers, understanding now how it felt to realize you were on your own in a place that seemed so foreign to anything you had ever known. With a combination of euphoria and trepidation, I waved one last goodbye at the car that couldn't even be seen anymore, turned, and walked slowly toward my house to start my life as a Peace Corps Volunteer in Mahon, Burkina Faso.

It's now two years later and last week I was the one driving away, being waved at by a crowd of villagers as I officially ended my service and said goodbye to the people who once seemed so foreign and now are so utterly familiar. My last days in the village were amazing. Although I always knew the people in Mahon liked me well enough, their warm words and gestures over the past week were unbelievably touching. Aside from imploring me to stay on and promising to do their best to find me an African husband, they showered me with thanks, blessings, tons and tons of peanuts, and five chickens! (My neighbor wanted to give me a goat and seemed genuinely disappointed when I explained there was no way I could transport a goat to the United States, let alone to the capital of Burkina.) Although no official announcement had been made, somehow the entire village seemed to know I was leaving soon, and thus I spent the better part of the week repeating *"Amina"* (the traditional response meaning "Amen") to such benedictions as: "May God bless your parents for giving birth to you," and "May God keep you in good health and give you many children." The villagers' concern and well-wishes for my family—people they had never even met—only underscored the warmth and hospitality for which the Burkinabe people are known. Aside from the constant benedictions, the villagers also had a request for me: *Il ne faut pas nous oublier....* Quite simply, "Don't forget us." For me, this was a request that was impossible to respond to; I did not know how to find the words to make them understand that I could never forget them or their kindness—that these people will always have a special place in my heart for opening up their village and their customs to me.

My last night in Mahon, the village threw an all-night party for me outside my house. Celebrations that lasted

until the wee hours of the morning were the norm in Mahon, and my closest friends knew that I had never quite
mustered the stamina for these events and was usually in
bed fairly early. But in the days leading up to the party, I
was told, "You are not going to get to go to sleep this night!"
And they were nearly right. For hours, we danced under an
African sky full of stars as the local *balafon* (traditional xy-
lophone) players performed their music. Later, the theater
group I had worked so hard to establish staged their skits
for the crowd. People kept asking me to get out my camera
and take photos, but I politely refused. I kept saying it was
too dark for photos and, although it was, the real reason
was that I knew pictures would never adequately capture
the scene in front of me, nevermind all the emotions I was
feeling. I closed my eyes and took a series of mental snap-
shots: the musicians' hands moving furiously upon their in-
struments, the circular conga-like line snaking around me,
and the children on the edge of the crowd giddily playing
tag the way any kids in America would.

The next morning, I awoke early after a few hours of
sleep. Mahon was quiet. I had never once been awake before the villagers (or the roosters), but this time, all was
silent as I put the last of my things together and I looked
around my little house. Soon, a small crowd had formed
outside, and 35 people escorted me to wait for the bus.
When the bus pulled up, I was surprised by my own emotions. During their two years of service, there are certainly many moments when Volunteers fantasize about going

home, about finishing service and saying, "I am done!" But now that that moment was finally here, it was a hard reality to know that I may never see these people again.

The Burkinabe have an interesting custom for goodbyes. When you leave to go on a long journey, you must shake hands with the left hand. This is quite significant because normally doing anything with your left hand is culturally inappropriate and is actually quite rude. But the custom holds that now you must shake hands with your left because it indicates that you have to return at some point to rectify this wrong. As the bus pulled up, my friend Clarisse held out her left hand for me to shake. I felt as if I had been stabbed as it finally sunk in that this was really goodbye. This gesture was repeated over and over during a cacophony of even more benedictions, more "Aminas," more pleas not to forget the people of the village, and mostly, my own repeating of *"A ni ce kossbe...a ni ce...a ni ce."* (Thank you for everything...thank you.) The bus driver finally honked that it was time for me to board. By the time I had said my last goodbyes and managed to load my things—chickens and all—on the bus, I was quite a sight. Despite the fact that I had worked hard during my two years to understand and adapt to local customs, this morning I couldn't help but break some of the rules. People in Burkina Faso do not cry in public. Yet, here I was, walking onto a bus crowded with startled, staring African passengers, crying like a baby.

Now that my Volunteer service has ended, people ask me if I think I have changed because of this experience. I may still be too close to the experience to tell. But there are little things I've noticed: I've gained a good deal more patience, I've lost a certain sense of vanity, and I've discovered the joys of eating with my hands and bathing under the stars. In general, however, I think I've learned less about me and more about the human condition. Burkina Faso is a terribly impoverished country and the sub-standards of living, particularly *en brousse* (in the bush), are something we as Americans could never fully understand. This is a country with more than 50 ethnic groups and languages, let alone a belief in magic and ritual that doesn't easily fit into our Western logic. But what I have learned is that, despite all of this, the Burkinabe are not so different from us. Babies get

born, children grow up, marriages take place, people die. People fight, love each other, develop friendships, have enemies. Some people work hard, some people don't. And at night, people go to bed only to get up the next morning to do it all again. We go through this life with its good days and its bad days and, ultimately, it is our relationships with others that make all the difference. The beauty of the Peace Corps, of this experience, is realizing that I have much more in common with a group of African villagers than I ever thought possible. John F. Kennedy, in creating the Peace Corps, said that one of its goals would be to foster a cultural understanding between peoples all over the world. To me, that goal, beyond any work I did in Burkina Faso, is the one I am most proud to have achieved.

Caroline Chambre served as a community health development Volunteer in Burkina Faso from 2002-2004. Her work included improving the capacity of her village's health dispensary and collaborating with community groups to promote health education and awareness. A graduate of the University of North Carolina with a joint B.A. degree in English and French, she joined the Peace Corps after several years working in the nonprofit sector. Caroline returned to the United States to pursue a master's degree in international nonprofit and public management at New York University. She currently works as the recruitment coordinator for the New York Regional Office of the Peace Corps.

TAKING TIME

Walter Hawkes · Tanzania

"You should do very well as a Peace Corps Volunteer. You're creative, and you have a solid entrepreneurial background," offered one of my dad's friends, a successful businessman, in response to my impending departure for service in Tanzania, East Africa.

"Thanks, I hope so. I really would like to make a difference."

And so do most Volunteers as they set out, I thought, somewhat naively. At the date of official conscription, my wife and I boarded a plane bound for destinations unknown to us; I was to serve as an information technology (IT) Volunteer, and she was to be a biology and health Volunteer.

As a part of pre-service training, the six IT Volunteers were assigned to internship schools. We were warned that, although each internship school would have computers, we were not to expect too much as computers were still very new to Tanzania. I was assigned to Arusha Secondary School and would be the sole IT Volunteer placed there.

As I was led into the computer lab for the first time on the first morning, I steeled myself in anticipation of finding a cobweb-infested computer graveyard. But to my surprise, I saw six, four-year-old laptop computers. They weren't bad either, having been recently acquired and refurbished. The week was going to be easier than I had thought.

In the lab I was introduced to Agnes, a young Tanzanian woman who had been hired to train teachers at the school in computer literacy. Agnes was very cordial and friendly. Even better, she spoke English and would be my counterpart for the week. Chatting with Agnes, while examining the computers we'd be working with, I quickly learned that she had a decent general knowledge of computers and was probably quite adept at teaching Microsoft Office applications. I thought to myself that this was going to be a breeze. We'd probably be able to teach the teachers most of Word, Excel, and possibly Access. The setup was accommodating, and I was excited.

Reality set in, however, when the teachers, mostly middle-aged or older, entered the room. I greeted them enthusiastically in Kiswahili as they made their way to the computers. Most of them looked at me strangely, probably wondering why a foreigner was in their computer lab. They returned my greetings with somewhat less enthusiasm. After they had taken their seats at the computers, Agnes introduced me as an American who would be with them for a week to help teach computers. Agnes then commenced with a basic Microsoft Word lesson. She handed them each an exercise to complete, which consisted mostly of typing some text and then formatting it by changing the font, making it bold, etc. The teachers began working on the exercise while Agnes went around the room supervising, correcting, and teaching—all in Kiswahili. I watched closely as to how she was helping and after a few minutes, I figured I could jump right in and make myself available to answer questions. One teacher turned to gain Agnes's attention. *"Mwalimu,"* she said. I quickly understood the word for teacher, so I approached.

"Can I help?" I asked in English.

"Mwalimu," she repeated, pointing at Agnes.

"I can answer questions."

"Mwalimu."

"Okay," I stammered while retreating, confused as to why she didn't want my help. After all, I didn't speak that much Kiswahili, but that shouldn't matter. They have to know English to be able to teach it. Besides, English is the official medium of instruction in all secondary schools in all of Tanzania.

Agnes finally explained to the woman the concept of selecting text, which had previously baffled her. When the teacher was satisfied, Agnes attended to the next person who needed assistance. Perhaps that was just the personality of the person wanting help. Maybe others would be grateful for my assistance.

Across the room I noticed two teachers trying their best to correct the grammar of a simple English sentence.

They went back and forth, both offering options. Here's my chance, a nice teaching opportunity, I thought as I approached. "Hi," I said. "Actually neither of these is correct. You can write it this way..." I offered, unsolicited as it were, two ways to fix the broken, but trivial sentence. The two teachers listened, gawking at me as if soaking up my profound knowledge of the English language. Or so I thought. When I had finished, they said nothing and went back to arguing, in Kiswahili, over the same points they had been arguing prior to my intervention. I hadn't made a dent; I wasn't even heard.

After several more similar instances, I became frustrated. Very frustrated. This is trivial subject material, what is the problem? Severe thoughts streamed to the forefront of my consciousness. Had I made a mistake in coming to Africa? How will I make a difference if no one here will listen to me?

Then Agnes announced that class was over; it was time for chai. I had tried several times to help and had been rebuffed, sometimes not so gently, in each of my attempts to teach, to help. I had failed miserably. Walking with Agnes, I broached my observations and frustrations. "Um, I'm not sure I'll be of much help this week, the teachers really don't seem to want to listen to me."

"*Hakuna matata,*" she offered, telling me not to worry.

I tried again to gain some insight from Agnes, forging my statement into a more direct interrogatory. Again she replied, "Hakuna matata."

I remained unsuccessful in drawing any more information out of Agnes on what I thought was the more pertinent subject at hand. Instead we entered the staff lounge talking about food.

"Do you like *ugali*?" She inquired about a native dish.

"A little."

I glanced around the staff lounge and took note of some of the faces that looked familiar, a couple of my Volunteer friends and all of the teachers who had just been in the computer lab. They had made their way to the lounge for chai. I became a little uncomfortable, a little nervous. Perhaps they were not particularly thrilled to have us there. But my feelings quickly changed. Agnes led me over to a table where one of the women who hadn't listened to a single one of my English suggestions poured me a cup of chai and started chatting with me in Kiswahili.

"*Habari za leo?*" She inquired.

"My day is fine."

"*Unatoka wapi?*"

"I'm from America."

"*Karibu sana!*" (You are welcome here!)

"*Asante sana*" (Thank you very much) I said, appreciating the warm welcome.

We continued chatting for a few minutes, as much as I could in Kiswahili with only a few weeks of language training. She was very friendly and social, curious even. Her true personality was quite the opposite of my first impression. In fact, most of the people from the computer lab came to chat with me at some point during that chai break, and each subsequent one, with genuine hospitality. The teachers became more comfortable with me when they heard that I could speak some Kiswahili, or that I was expending effort in an attempt to speak it.

Curiously, the second trip to the computer lab, for the afternoon session with the same teachers, was far different from the first. Near the beginning, two teachers actually wanted my assistance and listened intently to what I told them. I would have never guessed that teaching something as trivial as how to bold text would come to feel like a success after such miserable failure. But it did, although it baffled me. Why did they want my help now, when they could not have been bothered in the morning? What had changed? I had only talked with them a little in the best Kiswahili I could muster, very little as it were, over a cup of chai. Surely something so simple could not possibly be the difference. Or could it?

The first night I went home, exhausted, of course, and learned as many new computer-related words in Kiswahili as I could. It helped. The next day in class, the more I attempted to provide assistance in my best, broken Kiswahili, the more people wanted my help. This was great; I was really starting to help. And I did something else. I never missed a visit to the staff lounge for a cup of chai and conversation. Again, the more I spoke informally with the teachers, the more they would listen to me and, in fact, seek out my assistance.

I eventually came to call this informal time we spent to-gether "taking time." It's taking time to learn about teachers, students, colleagues, community members, their families, work, ideas, and passions. It's taking time to understand them, to become friendly with them, to care about them. For each of them matched my curiosity and care with their own, whether by cordially offering a cup of chai or by offer-ing something more profound like genuine friendship. By the end of the week, one by one, all of the teachers had opened up to me and let me help them. I wasn't teaching them anything complicated, just simple concepts on the computer. But nonetheless, I felt good about it. The last day, when Agnes observed that I was as busy as she was, she caught my attention with a knowing glance and casually offered, "See? Hakuna matata." I smiled, and replied to her wise words from the first day, "You were right, there are no worries."

Prior to this experience, I had been blinded by my haste, my unrealistic expectations, and my desire to jump in head-first in an effort to move quickly and make as much differ-ence as possible. There seems to be an unending number of intangibles in trying to make a difference here. The cul-tural divide alone is wide and complicated. Sometimes I feel lost at the start of a project, in trying to contemplate how it will eventually be accomplished and by what means. I'm feeling this now with the current seemingly insurmount-able challenge I face. Almost 1,000 teacher trainees and staff members are waiting patiently for computer training at my permanent placement site at the Teachers Training College of Korogwe. Somehow this needs to be accomplished using the college's eight old, barely functioning computers. I haven't the foggiest notion how this will happen, but I do know one thing: the simple but previously confounding first step—taking time.

Walter Hawkes and his wife, Melinda, served as Volunteers in Tanzania from 2003-2004. They joined the Peace Corps following careers in technology and teaching. Upon their return, they moved to the Los Angeles area where Walter is pursuing an interest in writing and filmmaking.

THE IMPORTANCE OF DRINKING TEA

Jake Jones · Morocco

Morocco is a country to be explored—as if by design. The number of hidden corners; the amount of diversity; the culture of hospitality and community; and the strong, continually changing landscape all desire to be discovered and studied. While I thought that my village was at the extreme edges of both isolation and charm, there was always one more hidden corner, one more isolated valley, one more rugged hillside that was more diverse, more distant, more alluring. So, when I could, I always took the opportunity to travel.

The regional trachoma drive gave me a regular opportunity to travel to even more remote villages. Trachoma is a contagious eye disease, usually spread by flies, that causes blindness if left untreated. Prevention is simple with basic improvements in sanitation, usually by removing areas that gather flies. The Moroccan government had instituted a program to saturate the affected areas with treatment and awareness-raising education.

I would join the jeep full of local doctors and nurses and we would go jarring along a road that wasn't really a road to the distant settlements, villages, and nomadic tents of the region. We would set out early in the morning and return hot and tired at night. It would often take two or three days to cover the whole region. The same process was used for the quarterly vaccine drives.

One site was inaccessible by car. We parked next to a sandy, brown hill and hiked 20 minutes on a high path above a river to descend into a wonderful green valley. Another site was a nomadic tent far in the desert, far from even the nearest village. Carpets were laid for us on the sandy ground to rest in the shade of the tent after we'd finished working.

Since there was no health facility in these communities, we sometimes worked from the local sheikh's house. We almost always began the visit with some mint tea, poured in an elaborate ceremony. The villagers came to receive their medication and instruction, along with a bit of socializing. Then we would be served couscous, eaten from a communal plate with our hands, followed by another round of mint tea.

This process was generally followed in every community we visited. Before the actual work began, we always had at least one glass of mint tea with some conversation about the local goings-on, regional events, and how everyone was doing. Then, after the work was finished, we generally had another glass of tea, some more conversation, then we were off to the next community.

It seemed to me that we could get much more work done if we refused the tea. In fact, we might be able to get to all of the communities in a single day. We didn't need to be rude, just a polite, "No, thanks; we have a lot of stops today" should do it.

"Jake, sit down and drink your tea. The villagers aren't even here yet; they just learned that we arrived." Sometimes I just received an impatient sign to sit down and not worry.

At one stop, a few houses were nestled in the side of a rocky hillside surrounded by small herds of goats scraping for what greenery there was to eat. I was delighted to see a generator-powered television and the host served us warm soda instead of tea. As I drank my soda and squinted into the fuzzy green TV screen, I became aware of the silence around me. Our host was sleeping; the rest of the household was trying to watch the television program, just like me.

I quickly realized an important aspect of our visit was gone. While the work was done in short order, there was no real connection between this community and us. I had been complaining about drinking tea before and after our work, but I saw that it helped establish respect and connection in each community we visited. I still have no other memory of that village; I don't even remember its name. I only recall that TV screen and the sleeping host.

As we got up and reloaded the jeep, our host gave us a sleepy goodbye and, rather than try to hurry home, I started to look forward to my next glass of mint tea and lively discussion of local gossip.

Jake Jones originally served in Uzbekistan as a maternal and child health Volunteer in 2001. Later he served in Morocco as a water and sanitation Volunteer. Jake then joined the first group of Volunteers in Azerbaijan, completing his Peace Corps service in December 2005.

BEEN THERE, DONE THAT

Stephanie Saltzman · Zambia

My friends always ask me to write a story about my Peace Corps experiences. I have always refused because I don't have the words to capture all the emotions, experiences, and life changes that come with being a Volunteer who served in three African countries. There simply is not one story that captures the feelings of despair followed by elation, of hopelessness followed by optimism, of self doubt followed by satisfaction of a job well done. How can someone who hasn't "been there, done that" understand my love of the rural African village and my desire to go back to be a part of the African village life? Or how much I miss sitting on my back steps with my neighbor's children eating fresh-picked bananas? Or how deeply I was touched by my next-door neighbors who, even as they struggled to support themselves, invited me for dinner every night to share what little food they had? Or appreciate all the experiences that went into my work as a small business development Volunteer in Africa....

I began my Peace Corps service as a Volunteer in Uganda and Kenya. I returned home for a couple of years to work and to pursue a master's degree, yet Africa continued to call to me. So when the opportunity arose to go back to Africa as a Peace Corps Crisis Corps Volunteer* in Zambia for six months working on an HIV/AIDS project, I jumped at the chance. After all, I knew what it was like to live without electricity and running water, I knew how to use a pit latrine, and even to crave foods I never thought I would eat. I'd "been there, done that."

My job was to evaluate the micro-credit program of a local nongovernmental organization called Harvest Help, which had an HIV/AIDS project in a district in Zambia. Harvest Help had obtained funding to give loans to women's groups whose members were being affected by the HIV/AIDS pandemic. Because HIV/AIDS affects these women on a daily basis, it is important for their survival and all the people who depend on them to help create viable businesses and give them the skills to sustain those businesses. Though the NGO had successfully given out the grants, it was having difficulty getting the groups to repay the loans. Many of the small businesses had failed.

I had learned from my earlier experiences as a Volunteer that taking a step back and evaluating was never a bad thing. So when I first arrived, I spent time assessing the different groups. Harvest Help staff wanted me to focus on business management training-of-trainers because that is where they thought they needed the most help. But

* Crisis Corps offers Volunteers an opportunity to return to the field in short-term, high-impact assignments that typically range from three to six months.

I needed to look at the whole program—from start to finish—to see how it was being run.

In one instance, I learned that the NGO had paid for
two knitting machines for a women's group from Chirundu
to make sweaters and sell them. Unfortunately, no one had
considered that Chirundu was one of the hottest places in
Zambia. When I went one Wednesday to visit this women's
group, they proudly informed me that they already had
business training. Then I found out this "business training"
consisted only of learning how to fill out a record sheet and
monitor time worked. When I asked about a business plan
and a group constitution, there was no reply. So we started
from the beginning, discussing the group and its objectives
and how a business would fit in with those objectives.

As we were discussing types of businesses and consid-
erations for choosing a business, the women realized that
choosing the right business and planning for it can mean its
success or failure. Hence the need for a business plan as
part of the application process—not just to assess a group's
business, but to make sure members have thought through
their ideas. This is especially important in an environment
where people often choose a business simply by looking at
what other businesses are around and deciding to go into
one of those businesses.

When I discussed the lack of business planning with my
counterparts at Harvest Help, they told me that the crite-
ria for loans in the past had been partially based on need
and, of course, with the HIV/AIDS pandemic, there is always need. From a purely business perspective, however,

need alone does not make a business plan. That doesn't mean that people in need cannot run a great business.

Once my counterparts realized the necessity of a structured process, it was not difficult to start organizing the loan program. We crafted a policy that would determine eligibility for the program, ensuring that the monies would go to the intended recipients. We created a basic application packet that included a loan application, a group constitution, and a basic business plan—all translated into the local language. Even though I had been teaching business practices throughout this process, Harvest Help now had the foundation necessary for its loan program to be sustainable.

Toward the end of my six months, I did another two-day business training in a very rural area. It was so rural, in fact, that we had to take a boat to get there because the roads were nearly impassable. During the group introduction, I realized that the group had been in existence for a year, but had no mission statement. Members could not tell me definitively why they were in existence and what their purpose was. So, before I could lead any business training, we worked on group capacity-building. We spent time defining the group's goals and mission statement, writing up by-laws, and doing some action planning. Only then could I return to my planned agenda and start what I'd set out to do—teach the group about building up a business.

As a Volunteer, I came to learn that you can plan and plan and sometimes things would work out accordingly, but more often than not, you would just have to be flexible. Though there were lots of digressions from our original plans, in the end, we still reached our goals more often than not. Had I not "been there, done that," I wouldn't have all the experiences, memories, and emotions that have left me with too many stories to tell and not enough words to tell them.

Stephanie Saltzman served as a Peace Corps Volunteer working in small enterprise development in Uganda and Kenya from 1998-2000. She also served as a Peace Corps Crisis Corps Volunteer working on HIV/AIDS initiatives in Zambia from October 2003-March 2004. She currently works at Peace Corps headquarters in communications.

ITAM

Jeff Fearnside · Kazakhstan

I met him when he came to pick me up from the Soviet-era sanatorium where I had spent my first three days in Kazakhstan, learning as quickly as possible some of the complexities of this vast country. I hadn't known a word in Russian before I arrived, and I struggled to properly pronounce my simple greeting to him and his wife, Farida.

"Zdravstvuite, menya zovut Jeff." (Hello, my name is Jeff.)

They both smiled politely and introduced themselves, but said nothing more.

It was early June, but already hot. The ride to my new home, a village on the edge of the foothills to the snow-peaked Tian Shan (Celestial Mountains), took two hours. Along the way, Farida stopped to do some shopping. While we waited, Itam played a battered tape of ethnic Uighur music, which I liked.

Here we first used the goulash of languages that would see us through the next two and a half months of my training—a mix of Russian, English, German, and gestures. Itam had studied German at university many years before, and

I had taken a semester of it nearly as long ago. He had picked up some English from his two sons who were studying it, while I took Russian lessons every day.

He always spoke slowly and clearly to me in Russian, which I appreciated. But, like many people, he also had the peculiar habit of speaking extremely loudly, as if sheer volume would somehow help me understand better.

"Jeffrey, come!" he boomed at mealtimes, his light green eyes laughing. *"Kushai, kushai!"* It would become a familiar refrain—eat, eat!—along with *chai pit* (drink tea) and *chut-chut*. Literally, this means "a little," but in Kazakhstan there's no such thing as a little when it comes to food or drink. Though Kazakhstan is a Muslim country, much of the population drinks, perhaps a holdover from Soviet times. While Itam occasionally enjoyed vodka, he did so moderately, and he never pressured me to join him.

I called him my host father, but he was only eight years older than me, so he was really more like a protective older brother. He taught me the finer points about local customs, gently chiding me for shaking water from my hands after I washed them (Uighurs believe this brings misfortune) and showing me how to give handshakes the Central Asian way—lightly but warmly, with free hands holding each other's forearms to show respect.

When I discovered that I had forgotten to bring a handkerchief with me, he gave me one of his. In every way, he made a special effort to include me in his life and the life of his family.

"Jeffrey!" he boomed. "You, me, go *arbeiten*." He always used the German for "to work," though I understood the Russian—*rabotat*—just as well. He was a veterinarian, and I would watch as he peered into cows' eyes, administered shots, and rubbed ointment into their sores.

Another time, he and Farida had me dress in my best for an Uighur wedding.

Ethnic Uighurs trace their roots to the primarily Muslim Xinjiang province of China and are closely related to the Turkic people of Central Asia. This wedding featured some folk music similar to that I had heard on my first ride with Itam. They also played Russian rock-and-roll and, more than once, the extended live version of the Eagles' "Hotel California."

At first, I felt shy and resisted invitations to join in the dancing. I sat on the periphery and watched, enjoying the seemingly bottomless portions of salads and appetizers that were a meal to me, though they were really just the warm-up to the actual meal. Eventually, I was moved to join the happy throng, the men in suits, the women in glittering dresses, their arms gracefully twining and untwining above their heads. We danced all through the evening and into the next morning.

The days moved slowly that summer in my village. It wasn't exactly a place that time had passed by, but certainly only fingers of modernity had managed to slip in under the blanket of time. My family had electricity and a television, but, like most of their fellow villagers, no telephone.

Water had to be carried from a well half a kilometer away; hot water was made by boiling it or, for outdoor showers, leaving a barrel exposed to the sun all day.

The family's fortune, if counted in hard currency, was a trifle. Itam's income barely met their needs. But as with Central Asian peoples since before recorded history, their real wealth was measured in the richness of their family life and in animals—in their case, sheep.

Toward the end of my stay, they needed to sell five sheep from their flock to pay for their children's education for the coming year. I was invited along to help catch them. We hopped onto a small horse-drawn cart and slowly clopped up the road to the pasture where two *pastukhi*, or shepherds, were overseeing the common herd. Itam's father-in-law chose the best from among them. Itam, his sons, and I chased them down, tied them up, and placed them in the cart.

Clouds of dust rose into the sky, the sun fell toward the horizon, and the nearby mountains faded into a hazy blue and then an indistinct shadow. It was dark when we rode back down the road toward home. I felt bad for the poor sheep lying next to me, but I felt good knowing that we were taking part in a cycle of life that had been played out for centuries here—knowing that Malik and Adik would be able to continue studying English, that Takmina would gain a marketable skill in learning to cut and style hair before eventually going on to university as well.

I also sensed that Itam was proud of me for helping his family in this way. My feeling of this only increased on his

45th birthday, the first and only time I ever saw him drunk.

He came in late for dinner, having been out celebrating with two friends from his university days. While Farida ladled out soup and prepared a pot of strong black tea, Itam rambled on, more emotional than usual. His family, unaccustomed to this, largely remained quiet. Finally, he put down his spoon and looked directly at me, struggling for words.

"Moe serdtse..." he said at last, pressing his hand to his chest. When I said I didn't understand, he repeated it in English.

"My... my heart...."

I was touched. He was trying to tell me how much he would miss me. I placed my hand on his forearm and squeezed.

My training was over, and the time to leave for my assignment as a full-fledged Volunteer had arrived. All the family came to see me off, all except for Itam. He had planned his vacation for this time and was away again with his university friends.

I tried to give back Itam's handkerchief, but Farida refused, saying that I would need it. She also promised that Itam would meet me at the train station.

To my disappointment, he never showed up. But I left with hugs from the rest of the family and more memories than it seemed two and a half months could possibly provide.

After a 15-hour train ride, I arrived at my new home, Shymkent. Far from being the dangerous place I had been warned of ("Texas" my family called it, for they believed it was like the Wild West), I found this sprawling, low-rise city colorful and friendly. Its tree-lined streets were cool and dotted with many interesting ethnic cafes. The university where I would teach was small, but its students were enthusiastic. I looked forward to a bright two years of work.

This exciting time was darkened by some terrible news: Itam had died the day after I left. Previously unknown to everyone, he'd had a heart condition, which became lethal when combined with his recent celebrations.

I remembered him talking of his heart and was shocked to realize he had been trying to tell us of feeling pains in his chest. In hindsight, it seems we might have caught this, but at the time it was the farthest notion from our minds. He was middle-aged and seemingly in perfect health. Only days before I had wrestled sheep to the ground with him.

I learned another hard lesson in hindsight when I found that I didn't have a single photograph of Itam. I had photos of the rest of the family, my Peace Corps friends, some village children, my pupils, even a few random pastukhi. I must have assumed that Itam would always be around, that I would have plenty of chances to catch him in just the right moment.

The only tangible remembrance I had was his handkerchief.

It's funny how small, seemingly insignificant moments in our lives can take on such meaning later. If I had brought a handkerchief with me to Kazakhstan, then I would have nothing to remember Itam by.

There's nothing obviously extraordinary about it. It's just a simple piece of cloth, probably bought at the local bazaar for a few *tenge* coins. Yet when I look at it, I see pictures woven into the cotton: I see laughing blue-gray eyes and in them the reflection of lush green foothills, snow-peaked mountains, dusty pastures, hazy steppe sunsets. And darkness. But in that darkness rings the clip-clop of horse hooves, the trill of Uighur wedding music, a voice booming "Jeffrey!" and I feel that at any moment I might stand up and dance.

Jeff Fearnside served in the Peace Corps as a university instructor teaching English as a foreign language in Kazakhstan from 2002-2004. His short stories, poems, and essays have appeared in Aethlon, Isotope, Permafrost, Rock & Sling, *and the anthology,* Scent of Cedars: Promising Writers of the Pacific Northwest. *Currently, he manages the Edmund S. Muskie Graduate Fellowship Program in Kazakhstan and Kyrgyzstan.*

AMERICA GAVE ME TO YOU

C.D. Glin · South Africa

It was about 7:00 on a Friday evening. Under normal circumstances, this would be my usual happy hour, but these were anything but normal circumstances. The rain pounding down on my tin roof sounded like a thousand children jumping up and down, stomping their feet. The gusting wind had long since knocked out the electricity in the village, and the strong drafts that crept in my room through the space between the floor and the haphazardly hung door made lighting a candle pointless. I could not go out and nobody was going to come in. It was just me, myself, and I until daylight, which would not be for another 10 hours. So I lay there, on my back, teary-eyed and depressed, contemplating all of the decisions that had taken me from a Friday evening of bright lights in the big city to blackouts and broken spirits in a little South African village.

How had I gotten here? The Africa part is easy. As long as I have had career goals, living and working in Africa has been a part of them. I wrote anti-apartheid rap songs in high school, interned with an Africa advocacy group, and even shook Nelson Mandela's hand at a reception during my junior year of college. My first trip to the continent came via the U.S. State Department when I served as a foreign service intern at the U.S. embassy in Ghana. Though this experience was designed to introduce me to the wonderful life of a foreign service officer, it actually turned into a recruitment session for serving in the Peace Corps. I met Peace Corps Volunteers my own age in Ghana who were having a blast. Not the same kind of fun I was having, of course, working in an air-conditioned office with complimentary maid service and a driver at my beck and call. No, their joy came from sharing themselves with people and having those people reciprocate, living and working in a community, communicating in a new language. Once learning about the Peace Corps life, I only had two thoughts: Why hadn't I heard about this sooner? And: Where could I sign up?

That year, President Mandela invited the Peace Corps to his country and asked for a Volunteer group that truly reflected the diversity of America. In 1997, the Peace Corps delivered the first group of Volunteers to South Africa and I was among them.

The assignment for this first group was in elementary school education, serving in South Africa's northern province as liaisons, advisors, trainers, and community resource persons for teachers there. The goal was to help implement a new national education curriculum that offered parity among people and would replace the current curriculum, which was based on ethnicity, race, and color.

Peace Corps training was tough at times. We were strangers brought together by outside forces. We had lived in our own insular worlds and communities in the States, but in training together every day from 8:00 a.m. to 5:00 p.m., we constructed a new community and our own support group. We literally grew up with one another as we re-learned how to talk, eat, and bathe in a foreign world. In essence, we were born again, born *South African*. Our training staff and host families were like parents, and we were eager for their guidance. I embraced the surname of my host family, *Myakayka*, a symbolic expression of their making me a part of their family.

I enjoyed language training and took pride in learning an African language, though it came with some frustration. After destroying one phrase or another in Northern Sotho, I would inevitably be drawn into the same questions.

"Where are you from?" Which really meant: "You're butchering my language so that tells me you're not South African, so what African country are you from?"

"I'm from the States," I'd reply.

"No, I mean where are you *really* from?"

"From the States," I'd say again, this time more emphatically.

Then came looks of confusion and annoyance. Why, they wondered, would I deny my heritage and language? Surely I was African. They would try a new tack.

"Well, where are your parents from?"

Having to prove I was not African always seemed humorous to me. And when the truth was finally accepted, my questioner, without fail, had a million-and-one other questions and they all started with, "Do you know...?"

"Do you know Michael Jackson?"

"Do you know R. Kelly?"

"Do you know Whitney Houston?"

"Do you know Michael Jordan?"

And on and on it went. They'd ask about any African American they had ever heard of and were quite perplexed and disappointed at my answers, which were invariably "No."

These conversations of heritage and where I came from often led to discussions about slavery and the number of people of African descent in the United States. As I gave impromptu history lessons, I always mentioned the similarities I saw between South Africa and the United States and the struggle for racial equality. Exactly 40 years after Brown vs. Board of Education struck down "separate but equal" in the United States, apartheid was struck down with the first national multi-ethnic democratic election in South Africa's history. I would explain that slavery in America was followed by a reconstruction period and the civil rights movement. I would tell them how privileged I felt to play some small part in South Africa's civil rights movement as it transitioned into a democracy.

The whole concept of volunteering and traveling to an-other country to do so did not make sense to many people I encountered. Unless, of course, I were rich. And, if I were rich, I must have brought something to give away.

"What did you bring us from America?"

"America gave me to you," I would say, feeling very proud. After all, I was a free gift to South Africa.

"Well, why didn't America want you?"

My abilities and experience were constantly questioned. In time I would learn to respond. But on this day, so recently out of training, I did not have an answer. I just stood there, blank-faced, feeling inadequate and embarrassed.

After the 12-week pre-service training period and the immersion of eating and breathing all things South African, I felt ready to take up my Volunteer post. Coming to live in South Africa had been a dream come true, and train-ing had only strengthened my enthusiasm. I did not feel as though I could save the world, but improving education in the small village of Phokoane I could handle. I knew that success would begin with trust, and before I could accom-plish anything, the community had to feel as though they could trust me. These were people who had never been told what they could do, what they could accomplish; it had always been what they could not do, where they could not live, and what they could not teach.

But my resolve would be sorely tested in the ensuing weeks. I would soon learn that training is one thing and real life another. I grew to understand that life's lessons cannot be simulated, but learned only by firsthand experience.

I was announced to my Phokoane community in the spirit of Paul Revere. The white SUV with the Peace Corps logo prominently displayed on the door pulled through the gates of the school, going as slowly as possible to avoid the little boys running alongside and in front, shouting: "The American is coming! The American is coming!" When the vehicle stopped, to everyone's surprise, out I hopped: big smile, dark skin, and miniature dreadlocks. They peered around me, over me and, if it had been possible, through me, back into the vehicle, searching for an additional passenger. It was obvious by the looks on many of their faces, that I was not the "American" they expected. As I went from person to person, meeting, greeting, and shaking hands, I could overhear grumblings about having wanted a "real American." I knew from that moment on, if I did nothing else in my two years, that just by being there, I would change their thoughts about what a "real American" was.

There would come a time of celebration. But, on this Friday night, my stateside party night, the only party I was having was one of pity, depressed and oblivious to the joys and successes that would come. Training had been comforting and calming, but now I was in the storm, figuratively and literally. With the rain pounding down on my tin roof, wind gusting in under my door, and tears on my cheeks, my only thoughts were: Why am I here? And: Will it get any easier?

Over the next two years, I could answer many times, Yes!

C.D. Glin was part of the first Peace Corps Volunteer group to go to South Africa (1997-1999), following the end of apartheid. His work as an education Volunteer during that period was enormously successful. After completing his service, he then worked for the Peace Corps in recruitment and marketing. He now lives in Nigeria with his wife and works in social marketing.

LEAVE TAKING

Beth Genovese · Panama

Arriving at Rio Oeste Arriba (West River Above) in Panama required walking 45 minutes down from the main road that runs through the province of Bocas del Toro. The community of Rio Oeste has 500 Ngobe indigenous people. Half of them lived in the center of the community, which was anchored by *La Iglesia de Cristo* (the Church of Christ). The other half chose to live farther out, close to the land they worked to produce root vegetables for consumption and plantains and cocoa for income. For the last seven months of my two-year service, I visited and worked regularly with 12 families in Rio Oeste, on projects ranging from business education to conservation.

Cata was the head of one of these families. She had 10 children and, like most Ngobe women, she was short and thick. She wore her long black hair pulled tightly into a braided ponytail. She had never cut her hair; doing so was considered bad luck. She had wise, sad eyes buried by a heavy, round face. Her unusually strong personality and sharp tongue was softened only slightly by her smile.

I visited Cata almost every Sunday, and we would talk and laugh as she completed one of her many household chores. The last Sunday I spent in Rio Oeste, Cata told me she wanted to show me parts of the river I had never seen. Dreading a long day of visitors and quiet goodbyes, the walk sounded like a good escape.

We set out at 7 a.m.—Cata was always prompt—with her son Gadiel and his friend, both in their 20s, and her younger, 12 year-old-son, Iscar, who was more commonly known by his nickname, Mudo. When he was a baby, meningitis had left him deaf. Although he was capable of making sounds, Panamanians generally do not distinguish between the deaf and mute, so he was labeled with the nickname *mudo*, which means mute.

I was guilty of playing favorites among the community kids, and I often paid Iscar special attention. I loved him for his expressiveness—loud in its silence and insistence. Whenever I walked through the village, he would suddenly materialize at my side. Smiling, he would tentatively grab my hand, squeeze it and let go—a release that always came too quickly for me. Hungry for praise, Iscar often appeared at my door to show me the grades in his school notebooks. Educating him was complex. Iscar was forever in elementary school because the second-grade teacher, a gentle woman who had taught in the community for over 20 years, was the only teacher in the school patient enough to find new ways to teach him. Although Iscar was practically crippled by meningitis as a baby, Cata had devised her own physical therapy routine, and he had grown remarkably strong. Often, I would see this boy who couldn't have weighed more than 70 pounds scrambling down from the mountain, hauling on his back 50-pound sacks of plantains.

Toward the end of our walk by the river, Cata and I sat on a ledge of rocks overlooking the water. The boys stripped down to their shorts and dove in, and Cata began to talk. The conversation meandered until she suddenly settled on the real purpose of our walk.

She turned to face me. *"Puedes llevar Mudo contigo?"* she asked. (Can you take Mudo with you?)

I wasn't wholly surprised by her question. I had noted that Iscar was dressed in his nicer clothes, and I had been asked half-seriously by more casual acquaintances to take their children and teach them English, to make them *gringos*. Still, I had not fully anticipated this request from Cata. Wary I might be translating in error, I asked her for clarification—would I, or could I?

"Los dos," she replied. (Both.)

"Technically," I said, weighing my words carefully, "it would be possible, but I would have to adopt him legally."

"Està bien." she said. (It's okay.)

So, yes, I could do it. But would I? *"Yo no se"* I said slowly. (I don't know.)

I was looking steadily at her, but I was thinking about the challenges I would face returning home after two years away. And, until I settled on a career plan, I would have little financial stability. Why couldn't I just say no?

Eager to change the focus of our conversation, I smiled and asked if she wouldn't miss him terribly if she sent him away with me.

"*Sì, claro,*" she replied. (Of course.) "But I know he would be safe with you; I know how much you care for him. You know he is intelligent. If he stays here, he will be in our house forever. We can't afford to send him to a special school, he will never learn more than what he knows now, and he will have no opportunities. The people here will only ever see him as Mudo."

I sat very still, quiet and pensive. With my knees to my chest, I looked at my feet. I could not take Iscar with me. Employing humor, a form of communication we were both comfortable with, I told Cata I wasn't prepared to be responsible for a child fresh out of the jungle with special needs and besides, Iscar would not fit inside my backpack. Although we both laughed at the image, I felt only pain because I did not have the capacity to help this child.

I knew Iscar was intelligent and curious and with opportunity he would learn and perhaps flourish. I wanted to give him this opportunity, but I felt there were limits to what I could do, and I wasn't sure that removing Iscar from his home, his family, and his culture was truly a solution. My experience in the Peace Corps had taught me that even some of the most straightforward challenges are, paradoxically, complex.

But I didn't have to explain this to Cata. She reached out, touched my arm and asked why I wasn't swimming. I stood and wiped away the tears that rimmed my eyes, shucked my black rubber swamp boots, peeled off my sweaty socks and dove into the water after Iscar. I signaled him to race me to the far side of the slow-moving river. He beat me by two full strokes and looked back grinning.

I have been home now for five months. Like Iscar letting go of my hand, the release from Panama came a little too quickly. I still feel overwhelmed with emotion when I look through the stacks of photos I have from Rio Oeste. I have told Iscar's story more than once and inevitably, someone asks why I didn't bring him home. The question frustrates me until I remember that I would have asked the same question before I served in the Peace Corps. It took me many months before I realized that my work in Panama wasn't about directly creating change but rather motivating change in others.

When I left Rio Oeste, the pastor thanked me for caring for Iscar and the other children. He told me that of all the work I had done in the community, the most important was reminding them that their children are their best resource. I left hoping that I motivated change in perception, in treatment, in priorities. And I settled for taking Iscar, Cata, and Rio Oeste home only in my heart.

Beth Genovese served as a business development Volunteer in Panama from 2002-2004. She joined the Peace Corps following a career working in various areas of small business development. Upon her return, Beth continues consulting for small businesses and is getting a master's degree in marriage and family therapy/art therapy.

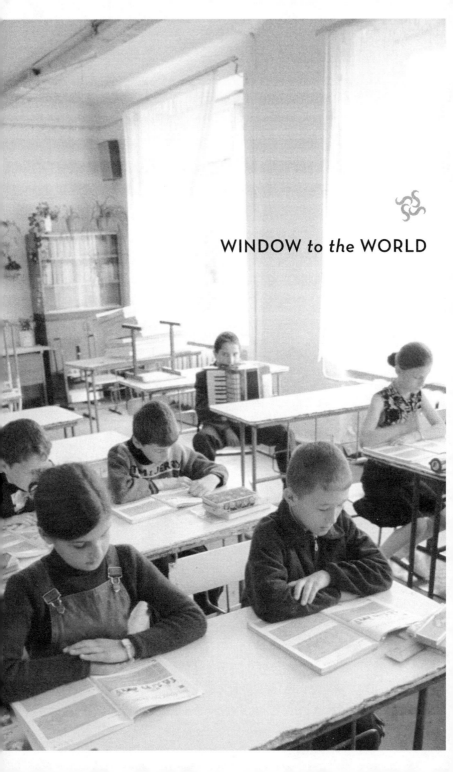

WINDOW *to the* WORLD

"The Peace Corps opens a window to the world for many people. I went through that window and became president of my country."

PRESIDENT ALEJANDRO TOLEDO
PERU

IF THERE'S ENOUGH FOR ONE

Kara Garbe · Burkina Faso

I didn't know what animal the head in my soup had come from. When Gara set the first bowl down beside the *forestier* (environmentalist), he pulled a slimy gray wad from an open cavern of bone, offering me first dibs on the brain. I shook my head in something approaching panic: me, the girl who was just easing her way off of seven years as a vegetarian. And while the forestier, the local government agent charged with enforcing environmental laws, knew nothing of vegetarianism, he knew enough about Western eating habits to enjoy watching my discomfort. He tilted his head back and slid the brain into his mouth, downing it in one satisfied gulp like he was taking a shot. I turned to my own dish. I had been gifted with the creature's tongue, a swollen cylinder lying purple over the teeth like a bruised piece of rubber. I looked from the tongue to the forestier and back to the tongue.

"*Il faut manger,*" said the forestier. "You have to eat. To make the *préfet* happy."

The préfet was the local administrator of the national government, by far the most important man in my village, and I was nervous about offending him. Eating food that's offered to you is a crucial tenet of many African cultures, and Peace Corps had drilled that into us during training. Since I'd only been living in my village for a few months, I hadn't yet learned to move past those seemingly carved-in-stone commandments and trust my own judgment about when it was okay to breach local culture. So, to make the préfet happy, I managed a few weak bites of meat (carefully avoiding the tongue), then pleaded a full belly and gratefully passed the soup over to the others. Their laughter as they accepted the bowl made me suspect that they had never really expected me to eat it anyway.

The Burkinabè had many customs around food that took me time to learn. (I'm just glad that my first attempt at eating spaghetti with my fingers took place far from my village, with no incriminating witnesses.) They also had many sayings. The most common one, which I heard my first day in-country, was the aforementioned "Il faut manger." To Burkinabè, eating well was synonymous with being wealthy and being happy. They often complimented me on having gained weight, thinking that my parents would be pleased to see pictures of me and the increasingly bulging stomach resulting from my all-carbohydrate diet.

Another common saying was, "If there's enough for one, there's enough for two." This could be modified to suit a group of any number. As I biked around the village, if I stopped to greet a few friends who were eating, they would insist that I join them. "Kara, come eat! If there's enough for three, there's enough for four."

Everyone in my village ate outdoors. Houses were used mainly for storage and for sleeping, and even the latter was debatable, since the oppressive heat of the dry season forced most people—including me—outside at night. Being inside at noon was even less bearable. My house had been constructed with bricks of mud and was capped with a tin roof that sucked in heat and trapped it in the darkness of my almost windowless home.

Despite all this, I almost always ate indoors, hiding like a fugitive so that visitors wouldn't come across me eating and expect an invitation. At first it was because I was ashamed of my nonexistent cooking skills. Before joining the Peace Corps, cooking spaghetti and heating up a jar of Ragu had comprised my greatest efforts in the kitchen. In Burkina, it took me months to figure out what to do with a tin of stale tomato paste and a kilogram of bug-infested rice.

Even once I had mastered a few decent dishes, I continued my stealthy habits. Since I didn't have a refrigerator, and the intense heat would spoil any food left out overnight, I only ever cooked just enough for me. It was true in African families that one more person was always welcome at the table because they cooked massive amounts of food for the ever-shifting extended families that populated their courtyards. But if you lived alone? I thought their "always-enough-for-one-more" mandate couldn't possibly apply to a courtyard of one, so I would sweat through every meal indoors, then bolt into my courtyard to take relief in the mere 105 degree shade.

Despite—or perhaps because of—this rationalizing, I began to feel guilty about my secretive eating. I felt especially bad about not sharing food with my best friend, Jules. After months of friendship, we had become closer than I had ever expected to get with a Burkinabè. I had listened to his reluctant complaints about the brother who leeched off his dwindling food supply. He spoke to me about the death of his first son and his fears about the mortality of his second. I confided in him about my conflicted feelings toward certain aspects of Burkinabè culture and my growing relationship with another Volunteer. He taught me how to raise chickens, and I introduced him to cheese ravioli. We discussed the existence of God and speculated about what happens after we die.

But our friendship still wasn't enough to break through this cultural barrier. I was thinking like an American, self-conscious about the presentation of my food: the taste, the appearance, the amount. Was the spaghetti overcooked? Was the rice under-seasoned? Onions, salt, and tomato paste were the key ingredients that I paired with my carbohydrate staples, and none of my dishes was pretty or tasty. It certainly wasn't guest-quality food, and, besides, there wasn't enough to go around anyway.

It was an accidental comment I overheard in the village one day that made me rethink my food-sharing habits. I can't remember where I heard it; all I remember is that the person was discussing a certain meal, one that he had had years ago and recalled with a nostalgic glow.

"Ah, that food," he said, satisfaction quivering on his lips as though the memory itself could bring back the taste. "When you eat like that, you can even get full."

Those are the words that stuck with me. *You can even get full.* They shouldn't have been shocking. I had been told during training that some students would come to school without having eaten for two, even three days. I saw the distended bellies and ultra-skinny arms that signaled malnutrition. Some of my teenage students seemed to be just muscle, bone, and gritted determination. Still, the intellectual knowledge that most Burkinabè were undernourished had never quite seeped into the reality of my daily life until then. The realization marked me: being full is a luxury.

That idea percolated in the back of my mind until a few days later, when I was planning to bike to Nouna, a neighboring town about 30 miles away. An hour before I was to leave, I had just finished cooking a yam stew of questionable quality when Jules arrived at my gate. I went outside to greet him, and we sat down in the shaded portion of my courtyard. We exchanged the usual pleasantries—how was the morning, how is your family, how is your wife—and then I paused awkwardly, thinking about the single untouched bowl of soup waiting for me inside.

Then it came unbidden into my mind: *If there's enough for one, there's enough for two.* Suddenly, all the sayings and traditions around food that I had been observing coalesced into something large enough to spur change. I was able to push it all aside: my embarrassment at the mea-ger portions, my worry that he would think it tasted bad, my selfishness at the thought of biking so far on such little nourishment. What matters is that someone who might not eat all day has something to put in his stomach, I finally re-alized. And what matters is a willingness to share, ungrudg-ingly and without hesitation.

My whole way of looking at food shifted. I couldn't take it for granted anymore: food was sustenance; food was life; food was what kept you walking those five miles to your fields, bent over rows of millet in the hot sun.

"Jules," I announced suddenly, standing up, "I want you to eat with me."

"Ah," he said, smiling with a touch of what I recognized as relief. *"Bari'a. Bari'a."*

When we had spooned the last drops of stew from our bowls, he walked my bike to the edge of the village and sent me off to Nouna. And what I remember, two years lat-er, is not the feeling of a merely half-full belly or the bland taste of my overcooked yams; what I remember are Jules's words: Thank you. Thank you.

Kara Garbe joined the Peace Corps soon after graduating from the University of Virginia and served as a secondary education Volunteer in Burkina Faso from 2001-2004. After her return to the United States, she worked for a year as an AmeriCorps*VISTA volunteer at an education-related non-profit organization in Washington, D.C.

THERE IS TIME

Casey Laycock · Bulgaria

In the States, I was forever on the go. I never seemed to have enough time. So it was that I found myself in a country with all the time in the world. Since then, I have been confronted with the two phrases that continued to follow me throughout my Peace Corps service: "relax" and "there is time." *Cpokoino* (relax) was the first word my host mother, Cici, spouted as I met her in the stomach churning craziness of "Meet-Your-Host-Family" day. As trainees and their Bulgarian host families jostled through lines to pick up luggage and medical kits and toss them into rickety, fume-belching Soviet-model cars, I frantically looked around, trying not to get lost in the confusion.

"Cpokoino," she reassured me and deftly maneuvered through the crowd like a natural. I felt like a wimp as I watched her effortlessly hoist my huge army duffel bag out of the pile and carry it out to her nephew's sputtering Russian hatchback. I felt even more like a wimp when I found out later that she was a diabetic with kidney problems and blind in one eye. As I ducked into the backseat, I almost felt sick with anxiety and excitement. It was Cici's smile that soothed my nerves.

"*Haide,*" she said. (Let's go.)

"*Da,*" I replied with a nervous smile as her nephew jerked the car to life.

Over rolling hills and past fields of poppies and sunflowers we trudged. Onward, past the edge of the Thracian plains and up into the Rhodope Mountains to the small mountain village of Bratsigovo. As we rounded the last foothill and looked across the small valley just before the climb to Bratsigovo with its cobblestone streets, red-tiled clay roofs and the single, golden-domed Orthodox church, it began to sink in. This was going to be my home for the next three months and the beginning of everything to follow. For a moment, my American "need for speed" disappeared. I wanted time to stop. I wanted to hold this moment like a child might hold a small, shiny bauble.

Cici's house was nestled against the forest. She literally lived on the edge of town, having the last home on the mountainside road that led upwards to the next, even smaller village. Often, I'd look up from my studies to see her returning from a hike, toting bundles of herbs, berries, and flowers; some for herself, some for her neighbors, some for her rabbits, and always, some for me. Always she'd greet me with a smile as she closed the wooden gate leading to her tiny courtyard. Sitting down next to me at her broken, plastic porch table she'd begin offering me the fresh, ripe berries she'd hiked down the mountain with. Those berries were sweeter than anything I had ever tasted back home.

Her smile seemed to say: It's good, right? I knew you'd like it. She'd laugh like an imp as I butchered attempts to say, "thank you" and "I like it very much." It was at one of these intimate moments that she told me that she wanted me to hike with her the next day. Like a normal, time-conscientious American, I responded with, in my broken Bulgarian, *"Ako imam vreme."* (If I have time.)

"Of course, of course," she assured me and without missing a beat she added, *"Cpokoino, ima vreme."* (Relax, there is time.)

The next day, my fellow trainees and I were told that we had a small language quiz coming up, and it was very important that we prepare. In American-mode, I fervently began to practice my Bulgarian over and over again in Cici's tiny, underground living room. I was so engrossed in my books and notes that I didn't notice Cici standing next to me, grinning over my shoulder.

"Gotova li si?" (Are you ready?)

Due to my classes and studying, I had forgotten our plans and I asked her "for what?" in bewilderment. She patiently reminded me of the hike. I squirmed, feeling terrible. I didn't have the time that day, but she wouldn't take no for an answer.

"Ima vreme, vinagi," she repeated over and over. (There is always time.)

I grudgingly slipped into my hiking boots as I thought about the upcoming language test and then headed up the mountain road behind her. I began to chide myself for not being more assertive. I tried to go over my lessons in my head, but as the gravel path got steeper and the foliage became thicker, my mind wandered from the thought of books and notes. On and on we trudged, skirting valleys that revealed all the colors of autumn, past babbling brooks, over the silent, stone remnants of Roman-era bridges, and along cobblestone roads with bygone eras etched in their deep, rocky ruts. I found myself standing in a virgin forest on a road that had once led to Rome. My mind reeled at the very idea of it.

It was a sun-ripened plum extended before my face that broke my meditative trance.

"*Yash, yash*," she grinned and laughed a little. (Eat, eat). Mortified, I suddenly realized I'd been standing stalk-still in the middle of the stone path with my mouth agape. I took the offered plum as she motioned for me to sit under the shade of the trees that grew on the side of the road. As I munched, I watched her move sprightly from one tree or bush to another, gathering oodles of wild figs, plums, peaches, blackberries, raspberries, strawberries, hazelnuts, and walnuts. When she returned, I asked if we should head home. Cici just smiled, resting her hand on my arm and said, "Ima vreme," as usual. I sighed and smiled back in agreement as we partook of the small forest feast she had collected.

We continued upwards toward the higher mountain village of Rosovo as we filled our bellies with all of Cici's gatherings. We passed small waterfalls, wild irises, and sunflowers the size of my head. I couldn't believe that this whole other world was virtually in Cici's backyard. On the way, she taught me the words for all the different trees, fruits, nuts, and berries. I was learning without trying. She would wink and smile with every new word I repeated as if to assure me that I had made a wise decision in coming and that she was much better than any textbook. Of course, she was completely right.

In those first three months, I learned more from her patient tutelage than from all my notes and grammar books. It took every ounce of reserve to steel myself for that final night with Cici and her son, Zaprey, who was leaving soon for college. She had made a grand feast of various Bulgarian delicacies as a surprise. She was excited for me that my site was in Varna, the "Big City," but I was reluctant about the change.

In all my time there, I had never seen her upset, nor cry. Every villager who knew I was staying with her would tell me how strong she was, how happy she was all the time. A mountain woman. Yet, that night I saw her strong visage crack just a little. That night I saw her cry. I was another one of her children, she told me, and all her children seemed to be flying away like little birds, but I would always have a place in her heart and her home if I needed. My heart melted. I felt something stick in my throat and tried to suck back the tears creeping into my eyes as I hugged her tight.

"You will come and see me often," she insisted, that mischievous smile creeping across her brown, sun-kissed face.

"If I have time," I said, which caused us both to laugh.

"Ima vreme," she said, finishing our little ritual, her eyes twinkling, "Vinagi."

There is time...always.

Casey Laycock served as an environmental Volunteer on the Black Sea coast of Bulgaria with her husband, James, from 2003-2005. She received her B.S. in marine biology from Texas A&M University in Galveston and joined the Peace Corps following a career in environmental protection.

¡QUE MILAGRO!

Kerrie A. Resendes · Guatemala

Guatemala City bus terminals were usually my least favorite places. Regardless of how quickly I could move in
and out of them, I still hated passing through them. The
bus terminals are some of the dirtiest places in the country. Bus regulations are lacking, and as they make their way
through the terminal, they carry the penetrating sounds of
rattling diesel engines, continuous blowing of horns, and
an indescribable emission of black exhaust. Although, on
this particular day, I did not feel rushed or stressed, the
stench was there, but not the annoyance; the sounds were
deafening, but not overwhelming. In this instant, I recognized that I had become nostalgic for all things Guatemalan. Who could have predicted that even my most disliked
places could fill me with a sense of home?

I made my way through the lively terminal to board the
bus destined for my former home, San Luis Jilotepeque. It is
in the province of Jalapa, located four and a half hours east
of Guatemala City and less than two hours from the bor-

ders of Honduras and El Salvador. As the bus approached the town, the familiar strong dry heat fell over me. I had not been back to San Luis in more than 16 months.

Unsure of what to expect, the warm hugs and sincere smiles surprised me. Within five minutes of being in my former *pueblo*, I came across countless familiar faces making me feel immediately at home. The women in the market, where I had bought my fresh fruit and veggies, sat in their same spots lazily waving away pesky flies and snacking on fruit. Their faces lit up when they saw me, and they came around from behind their stands to greet me. They asked where I had been, if I had returned to San Luis to make it my life-long home and, if not, would I take them with me when I returned to the States. I passed by the post office to visit my old friend Mario, the one person I was sure to see every day in the hopes that someone from home had sent me a surprise package full of treats. He took one look at me and exclaimed, *"¡Que Milagro!"* (What a miracle!) Mario said he thought he would never see me again, that I would never fulfill my promise to return. He was delighted to see me, as was the family of Doña Tina that lived across the street from my kitchen window.

When I walked into the *comedor*, one of two restaurants in bustling San Luis, I ran into Doña Tina's oldest daughter, Loyda, and youngest son, Walter. Before I ordered, Walter hopped on his bike and sped home to tell the neighborhood kids I returned. While eating, I enjoyed glimpses of the children passing by to see if I had really come back or if Walter had fibbed.

In my meanderings through San Luis, I bumped into Don Oscar, the *presidente* of La Lagunilla. He wanted to show me the present state of my wood-burning stove project. Luckily in my 16 months' absence, the government had finally carved a road from the pueblo to his village. I was relieved not to have to hike the hour and a half up the mountain.

To my surprise and delight, the stoves functioned wonderfully and have made a huge impact on their lives. The new stoves use one-third the amount of firewood, which has a direct benefit on the environment. Smoke no longer fills homes and women no longer ache from bending over an open fire on the ground. I remember completing the stoves, worrying about whether the metal stove tops would ruin from harsh sun and strong rains since a few stoves were built outside the home. To see houses built around the stoves that were once standing alone in the middle of the courtyard thrilled me, along with the community's sense of pride and satisfaction with the project.

I knew then that my service counted; I felt proud and satisfied. These feelings did not come from the stove project or any work I had done during my service, but because the community accepted me into its heart. I impacted the people of San Luis more than I could ever have imagined; however, their impact on me was far greater. I could never have predicted what my Peace Corps service would be like. Sure, I expected it to be bigger than anything I had ever done before, but I never expected it to provide me with a second home; a place that would become as close to my heart as my hometown; a country as familiar to me as the United States.

As I departed feeling like a town celebrity, I promised the people of San Luis that I would send them copies of pictures I had taken, that no, I would not forget them, and that yes, I would try to fit a few of them into my suitcase. I also promised Mario I would return again soon, even if it meant braving the deafening sounds of the dirty bus terminals.

Kerrie A. Resendes served as a family health Volunteer in Guatemala from 2002–2004. She joined the Peace Corps after two years of teaching health and prevention education for at-risk youth in Boston. Upon her return, she began preparing for a degree in naturopathic medicine.

HUMMINGBIRDS OR FAIRIES?

Megan Mentrek · Kyrgyzstan

It was the first of September and word had gotten out. The American was going to be giving English lessons at the community center to the public school kids. For pure entertainment reasons or out of a slim hope that learning some English might be a ticket out of the village, what seemed like the entire population under the age of 18 had turned up at my first lesson at my village's community center.

My Peace Corps assignment was to teach at a boarding school, but after months of being begged on the streets by students of the nearby public school, I decided to offer them a few limited courses in my spare lunch hour. I had not foreseen walking into a room overflowing with students eager to become fluent in English in a few short lessons.

A few days of brutally difficult lessons meant to weed out those hoping for an easy ride whittled the class down to a more manageable size—about 30 students. As I entered the classroom no longer facing the prospect of having to keep more than a hundred students in order, I breathed a sigh of relief.

As my eyes swept the room, my mind finally registered the presence of someone unusual: a middle-aged Russian woman with a shock of bright orange hair. She was with her young daughter. The woman's presence was out-of-the-ordinary because, up to that point, I had had only Kyrgyz students as I had learned their language to teach at the Kyrgyz boarding school. My Russian was limited to giving directions to taxi drivers and purchasing vegetables at the market. I had planned to use at least a little Kyrgyz in my English instruction to start with my beginner students. How was this Russian student going to learn?

Her name was Natasha, a jack-of-all-trades instructor working as the chemistry, biology, and physics teacher, as well as a stand-in gym instructor when the school headmistress demanded it. Her daughter was Vica, a third-grade student. In time, I would learn that Natasha was once a brilliant student of chemistry and shining star of the Soviet science world, a winner of the honored Gold Medal in Chemistry given to the best student of that subject.

At the time, however, Natasha was more a reminder of my frustrations. After six months in Peace Corps service, I felt no closer to unraveling the mystery of the art of teaching. I could not, for the life of me, figure out how to teach to a multi-language class or actively engage Natasha as she slipped more behind, solely because of my inability to talk to her.

In her plucky spirit, Natasha and her daughter stuck it out in the class for a month or so, but then quietly stopped coming because they really could not have been getting much out of the lessons. This failing of my teaching weighed heavily on my mind. However, all I could do at the time was to mentally make note to try to right my shortcoming at a later date, when I was less bogged down by work.

The school year flew by, and I still had not come back to Natasha. The opportunity to make it up to her finally came when I had to go to the public high school on an errand during the final exam period. She was there monitoring the door to keep students from loitering and disturbing the test takers. As I walked by and greeted her, I asked her if she and her daughter would like private lessons during the summer vacation. Her face beamed, and she agreed readily so we set up our first lesson for the next week.

When the day arrived, Natasha and her daughter came promptly at the stated time with a bucket full of strawberries. I thought this was a first-time thank-you gift and took it happily as my own garden was under the constant wrath of my host family's chickens and my next-door neighbor's turkeys. Little did I know that I would be kept well-fed until I finished service. Every lesson was accompanied by a gift of food. They could not accept that I would give lessons for free, despite my protests that I could not accept money from them. But I could not say no to regular bowls of raspberries and other delicious produce.

Because my Russian was still so limited, I attempted to get Natasha and her daughter quickly up to a level of English upon which I could base my instruction. This posed an unexpected challenge because I managed to strike about every fragile cord in Natasha's history with typical introductory questions such as: "What's your mother's name?" Many a lesson ended in tears and me trying to console her in my wretched Russian.

Everyone in Kyrgyzstan led an understandably difficult life. The country was not faring well after separation from the Soviet Union in 1991. I had not, however, seen this hard life from the view of Russians themselves. Cut off from Russia, often from their relatives who hadn't stayed behind after independence, and from the lives and usually advanced professions they had once known, theirs was a sorrow I had not yet been exposed to. Natasha was a window into that world.

As the summer progressed and Natasha and Vica picked up more and more, conversations became more meaningful and personalities started to shine through. Because of Natasha's inherent interest in everything scientific, I spent lots of lessons assigning English names to pages and pages of pictures of vegetables, animals, and insects. This was how Vica discovered my phobia of all things remotely resembling grasshoppers. They could send me into panicked flailing that would put most children into hysterics.

So, in one of my most memorable lessons, we sat outside going through an assignment on daily habits when Vica screamed out, "Grasshopper! Grasshopper!" She rarely paid much attention to English and mostly came to visit Dunkin, my puppy. After my story of my fear, though, she was sure to remember that word. I, of course, whipped around, ready to run unabashedly in fear. Then I realized that Vica was pointing at something zipping around the flower box by my window. A hummingbird! I decided to use it as a test of animal names. I replied "No, it's not a grasshopper. It's a..." and I started flapping my arms vigorously. She looked at me, perplexed and wagered a guess, "A bird?" I was thrilled that she had remembered and gleefully yelled, "Yes!" punching the air.

Her mother, however, shook her head, and said "No, Megan, there are not birds very small." It was true that it was amazingly small. After working in the Republic of Georgia and in Kyrgyzstan, I found that the hummingbirds of Eurasia are much tinier than their American counterparts and much less colorful. They almost resemble large, brown bees. But this was most decidedly a hummingbird based on its flight pattern and obsession with my petunias.

However, Natasha wouldn't buy it even after I looked up hummingbird in the dictionary. She claimed, "There are not hum-meeeng-birds in Kyrgyzstan" or anywhere in all of Asia. I did not want to question her in front of her daughter or demean her, as she was the village biology teacher. However, I thought this would be a good lesson for Vica to learn about the amazing flying feats of hummingbirds.

I tried to explain that it was a bird that moved its wings very fast. Vica marveled at this, but her mother persisted. No, it was not and could not be a hummingbird. Vica's eyes got big. If it wasn't a grasshopper or a hummingbird, then she knew the answer. "A fairy! A fairy!" (She had shown me a fairy tale book earlier and quizzed me on all of the words for princesses, princes, evil witches, and magical fairies.) How could I break her heart and tell her that my flowerbox was not, in fact, inhabited by a congregation of fairies? I left it at that and moved on to try to explain the magic of lightning bugs. Natasha, however, was posed with a challenge. Neither of us would back down on the hummingbird theory.

The next day she returned with a stack of biology books. I thought I was in for another round of what I believed to be unproductive naming of all things vegetable.

I was incorrect. They were books on birds. There, she showed me triumphantly—not one hummingbird listed for Kyrgyzstan. It could not possibly have been a hummingbird. I stood by my story, though. I just knew it was one.

The next day she returned, a little chagrined. "You win," she sighed. I don't know how many hours she had spent the previous evening poring through her old Soviet university textbooks, but she had finally found an answer: hummingbirds flew from Pakistan to Kyrgyzstan to avoid the extreme heat of Pakistani summers. They were not native to Kyrgyzstan, but they did pay us an annual visit.

I felt bad that I had been proven right, until I looked up at her face. She was completely joyful! Then I understood. This was a woman who once had been one of the premier scientists of the Soviet Union, but now was reduced to teaching chemistry and biology in freezing classrooms, with no equipment or textbooks, to students who rarely paid attention. This brief moment had posed a research challenge to her, and she was thrilled! She had learned something and had gotten to argue, and in English to boot!

Vica, on the other hand, was crushed to learn that fairies did not play amongst my petunias. As she had yet to see any solid proof that these so-called "lightning bugs" are truly insects, she was convinced that fairies with glowing rear ends at least frolicked in my backyard in the United States, and that was enough to satisfy her.

The summer continued in a string of lessons brightened by learning on both sides. I would never be able to cure the deepest sorrows of Natasha's and Vica's hearts, but I think I was able to provide a spark of something different. Lessons were a break from the monotony and difficulties of village life as evidenced by Natasha's words in a recent letter to me, "Your English—it is small light ray in my life." I could not hope to have changed the lives of every village member or to have greatly enhanced their livelihoods in just two years. But I can hope that I was maybe able to sand down some of the rough edges in the difficult lives that they lead.

Megan Mentrek served as a secondary education Volunteer in the Kyrgyz Republic from 2002-2004. She joined the Peace Corps after studying international development and international relations at Johns Hopkins University. She currently works educating students in global affairs and leadership skills.

CHANGING PERSPECTIVES

Christina Luongo · Bolivia

Thinking back to those first few months of adjusting, I remember the countdown I had going on in my head: *Only 22 more months to go... that's not so long. I love Bolivia!* It

was my mantra for survival, which would help pull me out of bed every morning. At the time, it seemed like the days just dragged on. I had yet to find my niche with work, and I wondered if I ever really would. I was just a strange *gringa* (Westerner) in an even stranger land. There were days spent staring at walls. Countless books read during the rainy months. Recipe experimentation to pass the time (by the way, butter-free, egg-less cookies are not the best idea). Rehearsing excuses to avoid eating yet another boiled *papa* (potato) or, even worse, freeze-dried potato known here as *chuño*. I always needed a daily dose of alone time to decompress and take in the new world around me.

Then one day it all changed. Suddenly, I wasn't the stranger trying to find a place to fit: I was adopted into a family of 137 at the local orphanage. Work, life, and friendship all grew into part of my daily rhythm. Time began to fly by.

And now as my days in the highlands of Tiraque come to a close, I have been spending every possible moment that I have foregoing the neurotic housecleaning that took up so much time in the beginning so I can hang out with the kids. Where the American in me used to say, *I must be doing something productive,* now I don't care if we sit around watching the clouds pass, as long as some of the children are by my side. I can't remember the last book I've read or the last moment I had to myself. I only bake when surrounded by tons of little (somewhat clean) hands, and we use whatever ingredients we are lucky enough to come by. I look forward to a plate of boiled papa, or any potato derivation, as long as it is eaten in good company.

One of the oddest experiences I had during the first month in my site was going to the wake for a man I had never met, the brother of the woman who owns the town stationery store. A neighbor took me because she thought it would heighten my cultural understanding. We walked into the front room of the family's home, and right there, elevated on a table, covered in a white sheet, was the figure of a man I had never known, surrounded by neon purple lights and wailing women. We all sat around the body and were served popcorn. It was a surreal experience—more like a night at the movies than a wake from my American perspective.

Three days ago, I revisited that scene. Only this time, instead of an unknown older man, the wake was for one of our boys. Tito, 15 years old, about to enter the fifth grade... and we lost him to suicide. I believe suicide is nothing more than a cry for help, but in a place like Tiraque, people are unaccustomed to asking children how they feel or what they dream of, and cries for help can only get lost in the blowing of the wind.

There was a time when the orphans were just a mix of smiling but nameless faces. When I was so overwhelmed with a new language, new culture, new life, that I couldn't keep a single name straight...and of course I was at a disadvantage because being the only gringa around, all of the intimate details of my life (true or untrue) were immediately known by all.

And now I really know these kids. Ana and Mari have shared their adolescent love lives with me while baking thousands of cookies. I am helping Limbert reunite with his sister for the first time in 10 years. I taught tae-bo to Hilda, Maritza, and Sulema; Samuel and Daniel taught me to dance cumbia. The teenagers and I have discussed professional opportunities and sexual health. We've celebrated birthdays and Christmas. I've given workshops to their families on gender issues and nutrition. We roofed a greenhouse at Wilder's together. We ate freshly harvested fava beans on the dirt floor of Filimon's kitchen, staying warm by the heat of the wooden stove. We spent days riding around the *campo* (countryside) in an overcrowded car, playing like a family on a road trip, while Isaac took on the role of family dad. And now we are grieving the death of a loved one together.

Every trainee wonders, "What is a typical work schedule like?" That question always makes me smile, because although I had a daily routine, I never really felt as if I was working. Chatting with the women and girls during club meetings, cooking with the kids, making sure their nutritional intake continues to improve—none of that feels like work. There isn't a day when I wake up and wish I could just crawl back into bed again and forego my responsibilities.

The crazy thing about the Peace Corps is, now that everything has fallen into place, it is time to move on. The countdown to the end of my service continues; but now, as I have just three weeks left, instead of wishing the time away, I'm trying to squeeze out every possible second.

These two years and these kids have given me more than I had imagined possible. Even though the Peace Corps had been on my mind since high school, I never conceptualized how it would feel to be at the other end of these 27 months. Tiraque has become a home, the people at the orphanage a part of my family. I've learned to love in a way more profound than I've ever known before—how to be an older sister, a mentor, a friend. These last two years haven't been about work at all; they've been about life, in all its depths, full of laughter and tears.

Christina Luongo served as a nutrition education Volunteer in Bolivia from 2002-2004. She then took a third year position as the education project specialist and spent a year supporting fellow Volunteers and traveling throughout Bolivia. After the Peace Corps she plans to pursue a master's and work with immigrants in her new home of Chicago.

DIFFERENT KINDS OF
LESSONS IN MOLDOVA

April Simun · Moldova

It's not every year you get a goat for Valentine's Day. My 73-year-old host mom misunderstood a radio broadcast that meant to relay that Americans often give gifts to their *animals* to show their love.

And it's not every day that someone stops you on the road and asks if, by the way, you happen to have any of your hair for sale. I chose to take it as a compliment. And I wondered if she would really want some of my hair if I washed it more often.

But then, this isn't every day.

Gifted goats and hair hustlers are the kinds of things that make life in my 2,000-person Moldovan village zany, crazy, and altogether interesting. (And that's not even to mention the fact that I think the majority of people back home don't really know exactly where I am living these two years. They know I'm in the Peace Corps. And most of them know the name of the country begins with an "M"— Morocco? Malaysia? Mongolia, anyone? But the correct name of

Moldova, the little former Soviet state tucked in between Ukraine and Romania, may or may not make their Top 10.)

Honestly, I can't say that I grew up my whole life dreaming of someday becoming a Peace Corps Volunteer, and in Moldova, no less. The Peace Corps made me think of places like West Africa or South America. Exotic places with grass huts and sand and excessive heat—even way more humid than in my native South Carolina.

But not Moldova. Not a place with unheated, concrete block buildings in the midst of snowy winters.

Still, here I am.

And am I glad I came? You bet.

Because the truth of it is that I can't really imagine any other experience that could teach me the lessons that Peace Corps/Moldova has.

There are the countless buses that never show up—lessons in patience.

There are the many times I make Romanian mistakes in front of classes of laughing children—lessons in humility.

And there are the scrawny bodies of hungry children who don't have mittens to wear in winter—perhaps the hardest lessons, the ones in gratitude and compassion, that still leave me unable to answer the question, "why?"

In all these lessons, I'm the student. Yet, according to my job description, I'm supposed to be the teacher. The lines get blurry sometimes.

My official job here is to teach English at my village school of 400 students. I teach lessons there five or six days a week to grades 5 to 12. My students are mostly native

Romanian speakers, who also speak Russian. But they see English as a key to finding better jobs and better futures.

My unofficial job spans far beyond just teaching English. It involves teaching health—giving information about AIDS, and why patients should demand clean needles at hospitals. It involves teaching about the environment—why littering is bad, why clean water is good, and why Moldovans need to protect their large forests. It involves teaching job skills—how to interview, how to give presentations, and even how to type on our school's old computers on days when the school has electricity.

Yes, the working conditions are tough. The school is old and concrete and not heated. Water is drawn from wells. Electricity may or may not work on any given day.

But with time, you can almost forget all of that. The children are children, after all. And the people are people.

Their stories, for the most part, aren't the kind of stories that make headlines, or that make Moldova known back home. Their stories aren't the stories of revolutions or of loud-mouthed, sign-carrying protests. On the contrary, Moldovans often laugh at their own hardworking acceptance of tough conditions.

But their stories are the stories of another type of heroism. Stories of quiet, unrelenting battles for survival, testimony to man's ability to keep on keeping on—through wars, famines, deportations, and economic collapses.

And from time to time, these people with their hardworking, persistent histories stop me on the road as I walk from home to school and from school to home. They stop me to tell me thanks.

They thank me for being here and for teaching their children.

And I thank them for the lessons they have taught me in return.

April Simun served as a Volunteer in Moldova from 2003–2005, teaching English as a foreign language. Prior to the Peace Corps, April worked as a newspaper reporter. April says among her interests in joining the Peace Corps was the opportunity to learn about another culture by experiencing it firsthand, which in turn would expand her worldview and enhance her reporting skills.

FOOD AND IDENTITY
IN AN AFRICAN VILLAGE

Allyson Gardner · Guinea

When I think back on the two years I spent in Guinea, West Africa, and what aspects of my experience there had impacted me the most, I remember the difficult yet peaceful routine of village life, the lush Guinean landscape, my eager high school students, the colorful markets and traditional clothing...but mostly I remember the changes that occurred as I struggled to establish an identity for myself in a small African village.

When I first arrived in 1996, everyone stared at me, and I stared back. I walked down the dusty paths and kids called out, "White woman!" By the end of my stay, they called me "Miss" or "Allyson" or sometimes "Sister." At school, during my first days of teaching, my students laughed and gawked at me. Two years later, they stood when I entered the classroom, and I felt I had earned their respect. Despite this change, or cultural adaptation, I would remain throughout my two years the white woman, the foreigner, the American, and I struggled to balance trying to maintain my own cultural identity while at the same time moving around in an African one where my roles were at best ambiguous.

The ambiguity of my situation—white, American, female, teacher—began to manifest itself most sharply in relation to eating patterns. At ceremonies, such as weddings and funerals, food was usually a main component, and villagers never knew how to treat me. Often I would show up alone, looking out of place with my Western-style dress and hiking boots next to their colorful *boubous*, head ties, and leather sandals. While most guests would squat over communal bowls of rice, sauce, and meat, and eat with their right hands, I was often given my own plate with a spoon and directed to a table to eat alone. I would sit there miserably, spooning rice and wondering why I felt so out of place. More often than not, the most important village elder would call me over to share a bowl of food with him. Still, I would be given a spoon and the best pieces of meat.

Closer to the end of my stay, at ceremonies I began to steal away to the back of the compound, where the women were busy preparing food and eating together. Each time my presence was protested, and I was directed back to the central eating place, dominated by men. With most villagers, I was never allowed that kind of intimacy, and although it frustrated me, I came to realize that what seemed like rejection was actually a sign of respect. By pushing me over to the men's side of the courtyard, they were, in fact, showing me respect. This idea was rather disconcerting to me—

what had I done to earn these village women's respect? I was a teacher to their children and a stranger to their village, yes, but weren't they the ones who deserved respect for their work so often overlooked?

The nature of food preparation in Africa, mostly women's work, involves processes that the Western world can no longer imagine: cultivating small patches of vegetables and grains by hand, pounding grains with a pestle as big as one's thighs, fetching wood and chopping it down for cooking, balancing large buckets of water on one's head and carrying it from water source to home, bending over the cooking pot in a tiny hut with soot-stained walls. I couldn't pound rice or cook a chicken, and every time I tried to carry water on my head, I ended up drenched and mocked. No wonder I felt uncomfortable spooning from my plate of rice, wondering if the women harbored any resentment that, despite being female, I was somehow exempt from this grueling preparation! At worst, I remained self-conscious during these large village gatherings; at best, my situation forced me to reflect and examine my position in the village, as well as the position of other women.

I developed the kind of intimacy and acceptance that I was looking for slowly over time and on a much smaller scale. I became an adopted member of the Dansoko clan, an extended family in the village. My relationship with them strangely became more intimate as my eating patterns among their family members changed. I remember quite vividly my first meal at their home very shortly after my arrival in 1996. Sory Dansoko, a prominent village elder and president of the Parent-Teacher Association, had invited me over for a meal. I accepted gladly as I recalled the meals I had shared with my host family during our Peace Corps training. During those meals, 8 or 10 of us gathered around a large communal bowl where we ate and took leave once we were full.

When I arrived at his home, Sory presented me with a plate of cooked liver drenched with oil and some bread. My stomach wrenched as I realized that I would not be sharing it with anyone, that, in fact, they had prepared it especially for me. I was relieved when another teacher passing by on his way to school responded to Sory's call to share the meat. Though disappointed that I did not get to share in a family meal that day, I discovered later that liver is considered the richest and tastiest cut of meat, and that by preparing it for me, Sory and his family were showing me respect and a welcome into their home.

When I left, Sory accompanied me to the entrance of the village and said, "This is your home. I will look out for you. Please come and eat with us, we will be your family." Touched by his kindness and hospitality, I thanked him and wondered what his motives might be for wanting to adopt me into his family. Over the course of two years, I would grow to realize how my relationship with Sory and his family helped me establish an identity in the village. I would show him and his family respect by choosing to associate with them. And, at the same time, he protected and fed me and allowed me to share and understand aspects of African culture that would never have been available to me were it not for his family's friendship and acceptance. Sory would even become my mentor when deciding on projects for work, and I chose him as my main counterpart for a public library project. A sense of mutual trust formed between us that lasted until the day I left the village and completed my Volunteer service.

I returned to the Dansoko compound often in the months following that first formal dinner of liver and bread. In the beginning, I always found a covered plate of food waiting for me at the table. If I arrived at mealtime, the rest of the family would eat on the floor together, Sory and his sons around one bowl, the women and girls around another bowl. Occasionally, cousins or other guests joined in when invited, and at any given time, there were between 10 and 15 people eating in the living room. I hated eating at the table—I resented being made to sit alone, isolated from the rest of the family. I tried to explain to Sory that eating alone caused me to eat less, so to compensate, he would spoon one bite off my plate and encourage me to finish the rest.

One evening, I took my plate and emptied it into the communal bowl and prepared to squat. Everyone in the room stopped eating and began to protest. Someone gave me a stool so I could sit properly. The boys crowded closer together to make room for me, and Sory just shook his head. I looked at him adamantly, and he realized I was insistent on sharing the meal with them. After that day, it was no longer questioned when I sat down to eat with Sory and his sons. I began to eat there more comfortably now that I had stopped being treated like a guest and foreigner. In time, I would abandon my spoon, despite more protests, and learn how to form balls of rice and sauce with my hand. Occasionally, sauce would drip down my hand and wrist; other times the hot rice would burn my fingers, and Sory would click his tongue and send one of his sons for a spoon. However, the satisfaction I felt, along with the sense of acceptance by his family, cancelled out any embarrassment I might have experienced over dropping rice or dripping sauce.

In time, however, I realized that eating with Sory, his brothers and sons, and occasionally visiting male teachers, was still a source of unresolved conflict within me. After all, I was a woman. Why wasn't I eating with the women? The first few times I tried to eat with the Dansoko women and their daughters, they refused and pushed me back toward Sory's heaping bowl of rice, sauce, and meat, just as the village women did at the ceremonies I attended.

During Ramadan, the Muslim period of fasting from sunrise to sunset, villagers broke the fast at the eldest woman's and man's house. The Dansoko women all shared their evening meal at Sory's mother's house, and surprisingly, I was allowed to attend. None of the women questioned my presence, and every night on my way out, Sory's mother would thank me for coming. It wasn't until Sory left for the Muslim pilgrimage to Mecca during the spring of my second year that I was finally allowed to eat on a daily basis with his daughters and two wives, Ciré and Ramata, who became the heads of household during his absence. When he returned six weeks later, he said to me, "My wives told me you were here every day and ate with them, and I am so happy. Thank you."

For my remaining months in the village, I roamed freely among the Dansoko extended family and ate wherever I pleased, most often with women. At the Dansoko family compound, I found solace and peace; I was accepted unconditionally, never asked for anything except to eat with them, my presence never questioned. I participated in Muslim ceremonies—baptisms and weddings, sacrifices and prayers—and gradually learned all the names and relationships of the different family members. My status as an American, a white, and a teacher began to wear off as I integrated more into the family, as my local language improved, and as I adopted more colorful and traditional clothing. But for me it was the transition from eating all alone with utensils at a table, sterile and unfamiliar, to squatting down with Ciré and Ramata and other village women in the outside kitchen, in the front yard, on the porch, natural and warm, that marked my acceptance and earned me a place in their large family.

Almost two years after my first encounter with Sory Dansoko and his family, I shared with them the traditional Muslim feast of *Tabaski*, where a sheep is sacrificed. After the slaughter outside the eldest brother's hut, Sory took the liver and grilled it, then offered the first morsel of it to me to taste. I grinned and accepted it, recalling the first time he presented the plate of liver to me so formally two years earlier. The rest of the family also smiled with approval. If occasionally I was still shown the respect and hospitality due to guests and foreigners, I had, at the same time, earned a place in the Dansoko family that allowed me to live comfortably with myself and others. A place that allowed me to forge my own identity—a combination of American and African values, amidst cultural paradoxes and ambiguities.

Allyson Gardner served as a Volunteer in Guinea from 1996–1998, teaching English as a foreign language. Upon her return to the United States, she pursued graduate studies in French and African literature. Since 2000, she has worked at Peace Corps headquarters in Washington, D.C., and is currently managing the selection and placement of Peace Corps Volunteers in Africa. Allyson and her husband, Mohamed Dansoko, live in Maryland with their daughter, Hadja.

HALLOWEEN IN TASHKENT

Ruby Long · Uzbekistan

The only Halloween parties held in Tashkent, Uzbekistan, are ones the Americans have, and if you see individuals on the street in a costume at that time of year, you know they are American and on their way to a party. There is no such thing as trick or treat. If you go to the neighbors, knock on the door and say, "Trick or treat!" they will probably look at you with curiosity or alarm. Not knowing what else to do, they will likely invite you in and serve you tea. Yet my most memorable Halloween was spent there when I was a Peace Corps Volunteer English teacher.

All my students, who were mostly late teens or young adults, had heard about Halloween and had seen pictures, but they had never celebrated it. They were fascinated and had lots of questions when I gave a lecture about the history of the holiday and described how we celebrated it in the United States.

One group I worked with pleaded with me to help them have a real Halloween party. "Please, Miss Ruby, can't we have a Halloween party? We want to carve pumpkins and make the lanterns."

I agreed to help them with arrangements for a party, but I discouraged them from trying to make jack-o'-lanterns.

"Your Uzbek pumpkins won't be as easy to carve as American pumpkins. These Uzbek pumpkins are much meatier; the walls are a lot thicker. It will take longer and be more dangerous than carving an American pumpkin."

They insisted, though. They really wanted to have this experience, and I was overruled. Several people said they would bring pumpkins to the party.

At our next meeting, I presented my plan for the party, which included apple bobbing and playing some old-fashioned American games like pin the tail on the donkey. After that we would have refreshments and carve the pumpkins. When the pumpkin carving was finished, we would light the candles inside them, turn out the lights, and I would tell a scary story in English.

I reminded them, "Don't forget that you'll have to speak English during this party. Just because it's a party doesn't mean that you can speak Uzbek or Russian. It's a good chance for you to get some conversation practice."

"We know, we know. We'll speak English."

"And each person can bring two apples for the apple bobbing and something for refreshments. But what about the pumpkins? We have to have pumpkins we can carve. Who said they would bring pumpkins? How are you going to get them here?"

The logistics of getting 20 pumpkins to our meeting place by public transportation was not a simple issue, and we spent several minutes discussing it.

Finally, I had a proposal. "How about if everyone who wants to carve a pumpkin brings one and a knife?"

"Good plan," they agreed.

In the tradition-bound Uzbek culture, there is little deviation in dress. You can often tell the age of a person within about 10 years by the clothes they wear. Certain garments—all the same style and usually the same color (lots of black)—are dictated by the season. Anything different is regarded with suspicion. For example, later in the year when I wore a Polartec hat instead of a fur one, everyone on the metro and the street stared at me.

So the evening of the party, when a lot of my students arrived in costume, carrying a pumpkin and a couple of apples, I admired their courage. For most of them, they had ridden public transport dressed like that.

Others changed after they arrived, and emerged from the bathroom wearing dramatic makeup and exotic clothes. Of course, through television, they knew about current monsters and space characters and some people copied those, but others used more traditional vampires as their inspiration. Two or three seemed to be composites of several horror film predators. Among the girls, regardless of their costume character, tight black dresses and long, bright red fingernails were the norm.

All of these outfits were created out of materials on hand, of course, since even the largest and most modern stores in town didn't sell ready-made costumes. The students gathered in knots, discussing their costumes in Russian.

"Speak English," I chided. "Remember this is an English class."

"Yes, Miss Ruby," they responded each time, then returned immediately to speaking Russian.

The apple bobbing was very popular, and noisy, with lots of screams and laughter. And cheers when someone finally emerged triumphant from the water, holding the apple in their teeth. They loved seeing each other get wet and without my supervision it would have been a big, wet melee among the boys. As it was, several of them nearly got soaked.

The girls helped each other with their hair. Lots of young women in Uzbekistan wear their hair at least to their shoulders, so one girl stood beside the other and held her hair back while she dunked for an apple. After she either gave up or was successful, they went in twos, threes, or fours to the bathroom and stood there, with the door open, chattering in Russian as they refreshed their makeup.

"Remember to speak English," I reminded them when I passed.

"Yes, Miss Ruby," they replied in English. But every time, the next words between them were in Russian.

I got them started with carving the jack-o'-lanterns. They all gathered around as I demonstrated how to get the top of the pumpkin off and the insides out. Then I left them on their own to design a face and cut it out. Not everyone had brought a pumpkin, so several of the jack-o'-lanterns were collaborative attempts. I listened as those groups discussed the design—in Russian.

"Speak English, speak English," I urged.

"Yes, Miss Ruby," they chorused, then went right back to speaking Russian.

It was interesting to watch what emerged from these group efforts and some very creative designs appeared. There were mishaps, of course, to both the pumpkins and the students, with several fingers getting nicked, and a couple of pumpkin faces having to be redesigned to accommodate knife slippage.

When the first pumpkin was finished, I demonstrated how to fix the candle inside and we lit it.

"Oh, how beautiful," the students exclaimed, some in Russian, some in English.

I had never thought of jack-o'-lanterns as being beautiful—they were supposed to be scary—but then I realized these Uzbeks, seeing their first real jack-o'-lanterns, were right. From inside the pumpkin came a soft glow. Those thick, meaty pumpkins shone with a luminosity I hadn't seen before. The whole pumpkin seemed to come alive and glow from inside like a giant jewel.

I moved from that group to another. They were still carving their jack-o'-lantern, and I helped them get the candle in. Now that they had seen what was in store for them, they were really anxious to have it finished. Finally, all the pumpkins had been carved and candles were inside, ready to be lighted. It was time for my story.

I went into the bathroom to wash the pumpkin goop off my hands and to think about the tale I planned to tell. When I came back into the room, though, the students had turned out all the lights and were gathered around their pumpkins. Each glowing jack-o'-lantern had a clump of people around it, taking turns telling stories, just as people all over the world have surely done for as long as we have had language and lanterns. And, although this was an English class and the stories were being told in Russian, I didn't interfere this time. I sat down among the monsters and the ghouls, the rock singers and the media stars, and listened to stories I couldn't understand, enjoying the magic of the moment. My story could wait until another time.

Ruby Long was an English teacher in a health program in Uzbekistan from 1999-2001. She joined the Peace Corps after her retirement from a staff position at the University of California, Berkeley. When she returned to Oakland she resumed volunteer work at a local elementary school and is also a docent at the University of California Botanical Garden.

THE TRAIN RIDE HOME

Robin Solomon · Kazakhstan

As my taxi slows to approach the train station, it attracts a crowd of young men who begin to run swiftly behind the car. Even before the taxi stops, they are opening the doors and the trunk to grab my bags. Since I'm traveling light, there aren't enough of my bags to satisfy the small crowd around the car. They begin to argue in sharp bursts of Kazakh as to who will carry my bags to the train. Hastily paying the cab driver, I jump from the car and wrench my bags free from the anxious porters. *"Ni nada!"* (I don't need your help!) I repeat, over and over in answer to their insistent pleas. *"Devushka,* 200 *tenge,* girl. Let me carry your bags!" In the end I resort to silence and take my bags myself into the train station. The frenzy of a Kazakhstani train trip has begun, and as I cross through the station doors and free myself from the porters, I have taken only the first small step in the 30-hour journey ahead of me.

As a Peace Corps Volunteer, I'm supposed to travel as the locals do, and in this country four times the size of Texas, the locals go by train, and so must I. With the collapse of the Soviet Union, the fairly well-developed air travel industry also collapsed, and nothing has come about to replace it. So when the need to travel is upon me, I grin and bear it for days at a time riding the rails.

It's really a lucky opportunity, I think to myself, as I weave my way through the crowds in the station—the grandmothers in their shawls and *valinki* (winter boots), the young merchants with their enormous suitcases strapped to the backs of sweating porters, the teams of football players in matching jogging suits, and everyone bundled up in layers topped with fur coats and hats. Traveling by train lets me see a great deal of this huge country, sparsely populated and filled with seemingly endless expanses of barren landscape. It's a wonder to behold, and a three-hour flight covering the same distance could never impress upon me the vastness of Kazakhstan's uninhabited steppe.

Once past the customs officer who wanted to weigh my pack, I'm onto the platform, filled to capacity with train passengers buying last-minute supplies, families and friends waving tearful farewells to their relations sitting behind the windows of the train cars, merchants with their hobbled porters hefting unreal-sized suitcases onto the train, and people selling fruit, ice cream, beer, water, bread, fish, and anything else you can think of. My journey to my train car is delayed by people jumping in front of me, insisting I buy their apples or milk.

Having succumbed to the vendors, I arrive at my car with a bag of famous Almaty apples, two *lepyoshka* (flatbread), a bottle of water, and some juicy southern tomatoes. Assuredly handing my ticket to the conductor, I climb onto the train, and I'm immediately greeted by a wall of thick, hot humidity that results from 65 people in an airless rail car for long periods of time. I gasp one last breath of fresh air and push my way into the sweltering car to find my bench. I travel in sleeper cars, as I need to lie down for such a long journey, but I don't go first class, where the sleepers are separated into compartments of four. Instead, I ride in second class, with double the number of beds and triple the number of people, without the privacy of enclosed compartments. I usually choose an upper berth, as the lower sleepers are usually taken over by the people without tickets, who opt to sit on the feet of the ticketed passengers who unfortunately chose the lower berth. On the upper, I don't have to share my space with anybody, but it's pretty cramped.

Shortly after getting on the train, we pull out from the station. The families and friends are still on the platform waving, but the vendors have already moved on to the next departing train. We roll out of Almaty and I settle into my bed for the journey. Outside the window, the city ends and the steppe stretches out on both sides. The stops along the way are few, but all as interesting as Almaty, filled with activity and bustle and, most importantly, fresh air.

Some small villages we roar through without stopping, and I can't help but wonder what life is like there, in a place with five buildings and nothing else for miles. I am reading a book by a Kyrgyz writer, Chingis Aitmatov,* who writes

* The Day Lasts More Than a Hundred Years, *translated by John French.*

of the Kazakh steppe: "The steppe is vast and man is small. The steppe takes no sides; it doesn't care if you are in trouble or if all is well with you, you have to take the steppe as it is.... Passengers look out from passing trains, shake their heads, and ask: 'God, how can people live here? Nothing but steppe and camels!'" As we pass the rolling hills around Chu, the red, rocky landscape around Lake Balkhash, the stretches of uninhabited plains before and after Karaganda, and the birch forests north of Astana, I wonder about life here, and the sedentary Russian settlers who established many of these cities along the train lines they built. The Kazakhs were nomads before the Russians established towns. Sometimes I think that the Kazakhs lived the way this land intended them to. It feels too harsh for permanent settlement. But modernity means staying in one place, even in the frightening emptiness of Kazakhstan's steppe.

On the train, apart from my own thoughts, I climb down from my bunk to squeeze onto the lower berths to drink tea, eat fish and meat, and share conversation with my traveling companions. They are always interested in my accent, and upon learning that I am far from home, they instinctively reach out to me with their Kazakhstani hospitality and offer me a boiled egg, a piece of candy, or some horse sausage. An old Kazakh grandmother hobbles to the wagon conductor to obtain a blanket for me, concerned that I will catch a cold, although I hardly think that's possible on the sweltering train. A funny Kyrgyz man practices his English that he learned in school 30 years before.

Two young Russian women traveling back home with cheap Central Asian goods tell me why I should come to Russia as soon as possible. After almost two years here, I've learned to enjoy this journey home to my site. The train, with all of its sweaty, noisy, and frustrating inconveniences, gives me an uninterrupted 30-hour reminder of the vastness of this land and the diversity of its people. The train reminds me why I want to be in Kazakhstan.

After 30 hours of traveling, the train pulls into Kokshetau. I know we're coming close because the birch trees line the tracks and there are still traces of snow on the ground. I see the hill that stands above my town, and I know that I'm home. Inevitably, some of my friends are at the station to greet me. They pull me out from among the bustle and crowd and hug me and welcome me back. In one shared breath, they buzz with news of the town since I've been away. I attempt to join the flow of words to tell the tale of my journey, but what I have to tell isn't news. Traveling in the train is something they know; it's an old story for them. For me, it's an experience limited to these two years. As I approach the end of my service, I know that there are only one or two more such trips ahead of me. And I can imagine that the train rides that I do a fair share of complaining about will be one of the aspects of life in Kazakhstan I miss the most.

Robin Solomon served as a Volunteer in Kokshetau, Kazakhstan from 2001-2003, working with teachers, students, and nongovernmental organization leaders to improve access to educational resources in her community. She joined the Peace Corps after graduating from Georgetown University, and she is now a foreign service officer with the U.S. Department of State.

SAYING GOODBYE TO PATIENCE

Ryan Wells · Samoa

I've never before had this feeling when leaving a place, especially a place that I have come to call home. I don't have any words to describe it. Strangely, I find myself able to explain it more easily in Samoan than in English. Of course I was sad when I left my family in the United States to join the Peace Corps, but it was only for two years. It wasn't the same as this emotion I'm experiencing now, as I prepare to make the trip back in the opposite direction. Part of it is finality, as if it were a funeral, as if I were about to be taken away for good. And yet there's still the opportunity to say what I would like to those that I will miss. "Closure" is the word that the Peace Corps staff keeps throwing at us during our closing seminars and workshops. "Make sure you get closure. It will help you readjust to life back in the United States." I guess that is the word for part of this feeling, but equating closure with saying goodbye doesn't encompass it fully.

One emotion inside of me is the same as watching a crimson Samoan sunset from Matareva Beach, the picturesque spot that was just a short stroll down a sandy path from my host family's house. I wish I could slow the sun down now, make the warmth and the simple tropical beauty linger just a little longer. But I also know that it is futile. The sentiment I have now is more like not knowing for sure that the sun will rise tomorrow. And even if it does, knowing that the students I have taught science and math to for the last two years will have either graduated or failed out and spread back throughout the islands or perhaps New Zealand. The school staff—my friends much more than simply colleagues—will have changed just as quickly as it did while I worked there. My host family will no doubt still be in Matautu, but Grandma is becoming quite old now, Sinapati has already moved to Australia, and Leilani, Vavega, and Iupeli may soon follow.

As if I didn't have enough intensity in my experience of leaving, my watch alarm failed me this morning so I am now racing to get to the airport to catch my flight. In my haste, I hardly notice the breadfruit leaves covering the lawn and the brilliant red tamaligi blossoms starting to peek out from the tree in front of the house. My taxi driver, knowing that I am late, urges his wired-together jalopy to go a few miles an hour faster, easing quickly through the normal stops. I see the capital city of Apia for the last time, not really looking at it as I instinctively try to run over in my mind if I got everything packed in such haste—passport, money, tickets. We whiz along the road that I now know like the back of my hand—every bike-damaging pothole, every snarling dog that is now sleeping in the cool early morning.

Now I see my old students walking to school, shuffling across the rugby field, book bags over their shoulders. The feeling that I should be stopping and joining them for the first days of this new school year is overwhelming. Then I see him—my year 13 physics student—a young man who lived across the road from me during my entire Peace Corps service. He wasn't a stellar student, but he tried hard, and he always came to my house and asked me questions that I had usually answered already in class that day. He is now standing next to the road, waving for the taxi to stop. I am so preoccupied with the possibility of missing my flight that I momentarily consider not stopping. My efficient, impersonal American ways are already seeping back in to take over the more relaxed lifestyle that I have come to adore in Samoa. *"Taofi fa'amolemole!"* (Stop please!) The sketchy brakes finally bring us to a halt several meters down the road, and when I get out, Onosa'i is running to greet me. Ironically, perfectly, his name literally means "patience."

"I thought I missed you. I just wanted to give you these." He holds out two *ulas*, similar to Hawaiian leis, obviously homemade, and places them around my neck. "I just wanted to say thanks. I never would have gotten into UPY without you." To get in UPY (university preparatory year), you must pass a test in all of your subjects. For Onosa'i to do it, he had to repeat his last year of high school after failing his first attempt at the test, and he had to go through the same physics class with me twice. I had met him on my first day as a teacher in Samoa, and here he is now to see me off. He flashes a brilliant white smile. "You'd better go, mister. You're late."

We shake hands and I half mumble something about him being my favorite student, but I don't hug him. I don't know why—some jumbled mixture of Samoan etiquette, American haste, proud happiness, and profound sadness. The taxi had backed up on the highway and the open backseat door is now right next to me. *"Fa Soifua,"* I say. (Goodbye.) Then I instinctively say, *"Toe feiloa'i."* (We'll meet again.) It's a phrase that had always been said when parting, but which now left me wanting something more.

Onosa'i is with me for the remainder of the ride to the airport; not the boy, but the word. I suddenly know that I will make my flight, and the chances are that it will be late anyway. Haven't I at least learned that much in two years? I finally breathe deep and just look out the window—really looking now. I see many more of my old students sitting at the bus stops, waving wildly when they realize it is me on my way to the airport, some of them coming into the road and waving as I look out the back window until they are out of sight.

I watch the villages pass by, fires already burning for awakened families, two young children picking up leaves in front of a yellow and lime green house, another child sweeping off the concrete floor of the ubiquitous open-air Samoan hut. At one point, the road gets very close to the water's edge, nearly touching it, just as the sun peeks over the horizon. With faint whispers of cloud around the edges, colors of baby blue and pale rose combine in the sky to begin the day. The water is motionless, reflecting every detail of the morning canvas as I pass by one last time.

It is the same drive that my entire group of Peace Corps Volunteers, all 20 of us, had made our first day in the country. The same time of day, watching the same clusters of villages, the same large, smiling people in sarongs, the same white-washed churches. But now I am going in the opposite direction. The excitement and nervousness of starting life in a new country has been replaced by this happy, sad, uncertain feeling of leaving. The most amazing thing to me at this moment is how little things have changed. The pigs are still in the front yards, crossing the road when they please; the clothes are still laid out to dry on the black lava rocks or in the bushes next to the houses; the mosquito nets are still raised in the morning to peer at the same sea and the same sky and the same Samoa.

There have been a few changes though, ones of which I am proud. One school and one community got to know an American teacher as a friend, one family now has happy memories of a white-skinned son, and at least one student was able to get into a university program that he otherwise wouldn't have. As far as I can tell though, the thing that has changed the most significantly, by far, is in the back of a taxi, on his way to the airport.

Ryan Wells served as a Peace Corps education Volunteer in Samoa from 1998-2000, teaching primarily science and math. He is currently at the University of Iowa, completing a Ph.D. in education with an emphasis on international education.

SHOWING THE BEST OF AMERICA
THROUGHOUT THE WORLD

Gaddi H. Vasquez

During my time as Director of the Peace Corps, I have been able to see Peace Corps Volunteers using their talents in countries all over the world. It is remarkable that the same spirit of compassion and camaraderie occurs with different languages, cultures, climates, customs, traditions, and values in the countries where Peace Corps serves.

Friends and colleagues often ask me what my favorite Peace Corps experiences in the field have been. It is difficult to pinpoint any particular experience because each trip is special and every country unique in its own way, but I never cease to come home amazed by the remarkable Volunteers who are integral parts of the communities where they live and work. Their efforts are truly making a difference.

One Volunteer whom I met in Madagascar is Nate Engle. He is helping his community not only protect its natural resources but expand its agricultural economy. Nate is working with the Farming Association to restore soil fertility to allow sustained agricultural growth for generations to come.

Initiated by the previous Volunteer at his site, Nate has continued his predecessor's success by creatively marketing red rice to Europe. By exporting this product, farmers are increasing their profits significantly and expanding their operations. Encouraging entrepreneurship and sustainability like this is one of the hallmarks of the Peace Corps.

The most gratifying part about visiting Nate, however, was walking with him down the main street of the town where he works, and seeing how the people in his community embrace and welcome him. Not only is Nate having the experience of his life, but the folks in his community are gaining a better understanding of America and our values.

When I visited Mongolia, I was encouraged by the hospitality and the welcoming spirit of the Mongol people as well as the productive collaboration between the Peace Corps and the Mongolian government. Mongolia has expressed that improving education for its people is a high priority, and therefore Peace Corps has made it a high priority as well.

I had the pleasure of meeting with Volunteer George Economides in Ulaanbaatar, the capital of Mongolia. George is one of only two Volunteers in the history of the program to receive a superior score in Mongolian language proficiency, which is no small feat. George is able to use his language skills to assist the staff of the Educational Advisory Resource Center in providing many programs for Mongolian youth, including exchange programs for students to study English in the United States.

Through programs like this, our Volunteers are empowering Mongolian youth by giving them language skills that will allow them to communicate with the growing number of countries around the world that use English. This will provide them with greater opportunities in the future.

I also had the honor of attending a swearing-in ceremony for a new class of Volunteers in Peru. All swearing-in ceremonies are special, but this one happened to take place at the Presidential Palace.

In his remarks at the ceremony, Peruvian President Alejandro Toledo said, "I can't be objective about the Peace Corps because the Peace Corps changed my life when I was just a young man." President Toledo was taught English by Peace Corps Volunteers who lived with his family. We can never underestimate the impact that the Volunteers are having around the world.

Creativity especially comes out in the secondary projects of Peace Corps Volunteers. During my time in Bangladesh, I met Volunteer Evelyn Ackerman who is a co-organizer of a tae kwon do class. Evelyn is earning her black belt and serves as a role model for the students, especially the young women.

Tae kwon do instills discipline, focus, respect, confidence, and strong character. Evelyn is excited to help instill these attributes in her students because they are not only key to the art of tae kwon do, but they are key components for international development.

Volunteers like Evelyn provide young people with confidence, hope, and inspiration. All of these are qualities necessary for them to succeed in life, particularly in countries where many times their opportunities are limited.

Survival is something that the millions of individuals infected by HIV/AIDS are striving for throughout the world. The pandemic of HIV/AIDS is devastating entire villages, and indeed nations, around the globe. The Peace Corps has never been an agency to sit on the sidelines, and we now have Volunteers around the world providing compassionate care and service to those affected by and at-risk for HIV/AIDS.

President Bush made a bold step in creating his Emergency Plan for AIDS Relief in countries struggling with this disease throughout the world. The President told me that he wanted Peace Corps to be a part of the plan, and we are honored to contribute to this monumental humanitarian effort.

Botswana is a country that has been devastated by HIV/AIDS. All of our Volunteers there are dedicated to working in HIV/AIDS education and prevention. I was so impressed by how the Volunteers are uniquely suited to do their work, when in fact the reason is quite simple. Peace Corps Volunteers live and work in their communities, they are trained in the local language, and therefore able to share information in a culturally sensitive way.

While some Peace Corps Volunteers concentrate on the education of women for the prevention of HIV transmission from mother to child, others, like Kevin Collins, are working with AIDS orphans and vulnerable children. Millions of children are becoming orphans as their parents die from HIV/AIDS or can simply no longer care for their children due to their illness.

Peace Corps Volunteers are uniquely positioned to work with these children, educate them, love them, and give them hope. Our Volunteers are doing an excellent job teaching orphans skills so they can support themselves, fostering support for them in their communities, and teaching them how to prevent HIV/AIDS in their own lives.

While the Peace Corps has responded to the needs of individuals and communities around the world, Hurricane Katrina in 2005 gave us the opportunity to ease the suffering of our fellow Americans at home.

In the finest tradition of the Peace Corps, we signed an agreement with the Federal Emergency Management Agency to provide our Crisis Corps Volunteers to support the emergency relief operation in the hurricane-devastated Gulf Coast region. I toured the area several weeks after the storm, and I was able to see the remarkable work our Crisis Corps Volunteers were doing in Louisiana.

One Volunteer, Ballard Krudop, is a New Orleans resident who sustained flooding in his own home. Our team visited his home to see the damage. In true Peace Corps style, Ballard put his own personal tragedy aside to work at one of the disaster recovery centers.

Another Volunteer from New Orleans, Sarah Ashe, also sustained damage to her own home. She told her husband that she may not be good with a hammer, but she knew how to volunteer. So, while he repaired their house, she helped folks complete assistance applications at another disaster recovery center.

I could not be more proud of the difference that the Peace Corps is making throughout the world, but none of it would be possible without the giving nature of our Volunteers. While I am fond of saying that the Peace Corps represents the best that America has to offer, it is a fact that our Volunteers are the most precious resource of the Peace Corps.

I wish that every member of the Peace Corps family could meet the thousands of Volunteers throughout the world that I have.

The work our Volunteers do each day is inspiring. During my visits with heads of state throughout the world, they all tell me how much they appreciate the Peace Corps, and how they want to see more of our Volunteers working in their countries.

While the Peace Corps has changed and grown since its creation in 1961 to meet the challenges of our times and a global marketplace, it has never swayed from its mission. I am grateful to President Bush for his support of Peace Corps, of me, and of his desire to see the Peace Corps expand and flourish in the years to come. He knows, as I do, that our Peace Corps Volunteers are the face of America to millions throughout the world.

Gaddi H. Vasquez is the 16th Director of the Peace Corps.

HEIGHT OF MENENGAI 2272 M.
AREA OF CRATER 90 SQ KM.
DEPTH OF CRATER 485 M.
DISTANCES ARE IN KM.

LAKE TURKANA
3542 CAIRO
5997 ROME
6924 LONDON
12360 NEW YORK
13687 EVANSTON
53 MT. LONDIANI
389 KAMPALA
2416 KINSHASA

MT. KILIMANJARO 346
DAR ES SALAAM 821
NAIROBI 148
LAKE ELMENTAITA 28
MOMBASA 579
ABERDARES 72
MT. KENYA 138

LUSAKA 1816
CAPE TOWN 4186
HARARE 1932

BECOMING A
PEACE CORPS VOLUNTEER

Since its inception, the Peace Corps has aimed to promote world peace and friendship by:

- helping the people of interested countries in meeting their need for trained men and women

- helping promote a better understanding of Americans on the part of the peoples served

- helping promote a better understanding of other peoples on the part of Americans

One of the goals of the Peace Corps is to help the people of other countries gain a better understanding of Americans and our multicultural society. The agency actively recruits people with a variety of backgrounds and experiences to best share the nation's greatest resource—its people—with the communities where Volunteers serve around the globe. The Peace Corps welcomes people from every background and does not discriminate against anyone because of race, color, national origin, religion, age, sex, disability, political affiliation, sexual orientation, marital status, or union membership.

Are you inspired?

Consider becoming a Peace Corps Volunteer.

Learn more by talking to
a Peace Corps recruiter.

Call 800.424.8580 or visit www.peacecorps.gov

This map shows the 23 countries featured in
the stories in *A Life Inspired*. It is not to scale.

KAZAKHSTAN

UZBEKISTAN KYRGYZSTAN

NEPAL

SAMOA

177